The Impressionists

Gilles Néret

The Impressionists

TIGER BOOKS INTERNATIONAL

LONDON

This edition published in 1992 by
Tiger Books International PLC, London

© 1985 Office du Livre S.A., Fribourg, Switzerland

Translated by Kit Currie.

English translation copyright © 1988 by
William S. Konecky Associates, Inc.

Published by special arrangement with
William S. Konecky Associates, Inc.

ISBN: 1-85501-240-5

Printed in China

Table of Contents

I	Obsessed by light	7
II	The superior genre	24
III	The spleen of Paris	41
IV	The tools of labor	55
V	The artificial life	65
VI	Water, reflection of a reflection	75
VII	Weather landscapes	93
VIII	The portrait king	105
IX	Venus or Nini	129
X	Shrines of femininity	139
XI	Through the wall of intimacy	143
XII	Still life	147
List of illustrations		156
Bibliography		158

I   Obsessed by light

"I'm well aware," said Renoir, "that it's difficult to acknowledge that a painting can be both great and yet full of fun. Because Fragonard made jokes, people were quick to say he was a secondary artist. Those who laugh aren't taken seriously. But art in formal dress, whether it's painting, music, or literature, will always impress us." The crowds who stand in long lines to see Impressionist exhibitions today—at a time when a smile is a rare thing—seem to acknowledge that this painter of happiness was right.

However, these ten or so "madmen" who managed to focus such official hostility upon themselves during the twenty years (1860-1880) of the Impressionist adventure, had much else to be forgiven for. One doesn't flout the most firmly established rules of western art without causing dismay and astonishment. One doesn't aspire to have hanging in the Salons what seems at first glance a rough sketch, splattered with blobs, or outlines traced with a light brush, when the glossy and perfected are proof of art and of serious work. One doesn't sit at a bridge table to play poker. The members of the Institut, the Beaux-Arts professors, are in absolute good faith when they write, like Gérôme, immortal creator of the *Death of Caesar* and the *Reception of the Duke of Condé at Versailles*, in 1894, "Painting will be finished under them, I tell you. They joke, they say, 'Oh, it's nothing,' but you wait and see, it will be the end of the country, the end of France."

Nevertheless these "angry young men" had the best intentions. Worse yet, they came from good families. They were rather like those very well-born sons of Neuilly who are found on the extreme left. Bazille came from an old, rich, Protestant family, Degas was born in the bosom of the financial aristocracy, Manet's father was a high official, and Cézanne's was a banker. The parents of Monet and Pissarro were merchants in easy circumstances. Caillebotte had an industrialist for a father, and Berthe Morisot a magistrate. Only Renoir came from a poor family. The rich bourgeois Manet, elegant, sociable, something of a snob, steeped in tradition, respectful of the past, only wanted people to like him, to attain critical and public recognition. He sought official glory, and favor and medals from the Salons. He unintentionally provoked scandal after scandal, while trying to excuse himself: "Sincerity gives to painting a character of protest, while in fact, the artist simply wants to render his idea. He wants only to be himself. He says 'sincerity' and people cry 'indecency.'"

Manet summed up all his work with a command that future generations would follow: "Look for bright light and deep shadow, the rest will come naturally, and it's often little enough." A slight remark yet it weighs heavily enough in the working out of contemporary painting. In contrast to the Neo-Classicists who overwhelm a picture with forms and lifelike figures which stand out from the background, the Impressionists see a picture as a blend of colored splashes forming a whole in which landscape and figures are merged.

The Impressionists were not scholars, but they had some knowledge of the work of the chemist Chevreul. Having observed that the juxtaposition of colored objects modified the optical nature of them, Chevreul, director of the Gobelin tapestry works, formulated the Law of Simultaneous Color Contrasts. This law may be summed up in two points: each color tends to tint with its complementary color its neighboring colors; if two objects contain a common color, the effect of their juxtaposition is to lessen the intensity of the common element. Thus, with science supporting their own empirical discoveries, the

1   **Pierre-Auguste Renoir:** *The Swing.* **1876. Oil on canvas, 92 x 73 cm. Paris, Musée d'Orsay, Galerie du Jeu de Paume**

While living in Montmartre, Renoir worked simultaneously on *Le Moulin de la Galette* and *The Swing*. With these two works he was able to produce something new out of an everyday scene, rendering the ordinary as fresh and surprising. By the juxtaposition of brightly colored strokes of color he was able to reproduce the effects of dappled sunlight piercing the foliage.

Impressionists boldly ventured forth. The day would come when the Neo-Impressionists, with Seurat, would try to make an equation of the magic formula.

For the time being the Impressionists were content to be nothing but an eye. "But what an eye!" Cézanne would say to Monet. To a friend who quoted to him Amiel's idea that "a landscape is a state of soul," Degas answered, "Oh no, a landscape is a state of eye." The traditional conventions were abandoned: drawing, perspective, studio lighting. The thing was to suggest form and distance by their own vibrations and color contrasts. "I have spent my life 'knitting prisms,'" Monet would say, "treating light like a piece of embroidery."

At that time the fashion for landscape was at its zenith in Europe. English artists invaded Chamonix and Pau each summer. The forests of the Serpentara near Rome, and of Soignes near Brussels were veritable open-air studios. The forest of Fontainebleau, if the Goncourt brothers are to be believed, was full of bearded young painters without any money, carrying their easels on their backs. Against the shameless display of riches and bourgeois bad taste, the Impressionists reacted as ecologists. Sisley and Renoir were at Barbizon, Monet and Bazille at Chailly-en-Bière. "No self-respecting painter should touch a brush if his model isn't under his eyes," Diaz had said to them. True Parisians, they left Paris for the country. "He cannot paint a landscape without putting in dressed-up ladies and gentlemen," Zola wrote in an article entitled "Claude Monet, Modern Painter."

Responding to those who were astonished that his picture *Women in the Garden* (ill. 9) had been painted in the open air despite its large size (2.55 x 2.05 m.), Monet remarked: "Yes, I really painted this picture on the spot and from nature, which wasn't previously done. I scooped out a hole in the ground, a sort of ditch, into which I could progressively lower my canvas as I reached the top." What he didn't reveal is that he had employed only his first wife, Camille, and a friend to represent the four young women dressed in elegant summer dresses. He used fashion engravings for the costumes and had gone over each part carefully in the studio. The faces are surprising; drawn like masks and already approaching the abstract, they are even more stylized than some figures of Manet. For *Women in the Garden* is also a challenge to Manet. Monet meant to prove that he was not only a landscape artist, but could also put figures into them.

Manet was already in the limelight because of a scandal which everyone was talking about for better, but mostly for worse. "It seems that I must do a nude," he had said at Argenteuil. "Well, I'm going to do one in a transparent atmosphere with people like those you see down there. They are going to tear me to pieces. Let them say what they like!" Manet sent his *Luncheon on the Grass* (ill. 4) to the Salon, hoping for a medal. But, as he had predicted, they did tear him to pieces. However, he had taken some precautions. Knowing that he would have some trouble he had taken his composition straight from Titian and Raphael. Nothing could be more classical. But this more than a naked woman, rendered even more immodest by the proximity of the fully clothed men, had the effect of a stone thrown into a pond. Manet's intentions had not been altogether innocent. He himself had spoken of its being a *partie carrée*, a pleasure party for four. Delacroix's nudes are always more or less idealized, and those of Courbet, even the most licentious, are not completely detached from academic conventions. This woman, undressed rather than naked, gives the effect of a photograph taken by a prying camera. Thus Manet "blackmailed" the hypocritical bourgeoisie of his time, who could not bear such a scene, astonishingly modern, far from any mythological pretext, the subject and the technique both running counter to precedent and behavior. In *Le Figaro* of 24 May 1863, Charles Monselet wrote: "M. Manet is a pupil of Goya and Baudelaire. He has already gained the disgust of the middle class."

Courbet himself, that "painter of the low" who had been given the title of realist and whose *Young Women on the Bank of the Seine* (ill. 2) had partly inspired *Luncheon on the Grass,* had not been as calm a revolutionary. Certainly the critics had bitterly attacked his picture for its "subject of doubtful taste." He had overturned a longstanding convention: only nymphs are supposed to haunt the riverside. Courbet meant it to be clearly understood that these "young

2 **Gustave Courbet:** *Young Women on the Banks of the Seine.* **Summer 1856. Oil on canvas, 174 x 206 cm. Paris, Musée du Petit Palais**

3 **Eugène Delacroix:** *Death of Ophelia.* **1843. Oil on canvas, 23 x 30.5 cm. Paris, The Louvre**

The two elders of Impressionism. Courbet, the "Realist" replaced the academic nymphs by young women of doubtful virtue; Delacroix, the "Romanticist" began the division of color into tones, and the colored vibrations of *Ophelia* anticipate those of *Nini.*

ladies" obviously of loose morals, these "working girls" dressed in their Sunday best, had not merely passed the afternoon in gathering flowers. Stupendous in execution, teeming with an assortment of things (the clothes, the bunch of flowers, the mittens of the big girl), *Young Women* is already Impressionist.

In the same way Delacroix, with his *Death of Ophelia* (ill. 3), is halfway between Romanticism and Impressionism. This "painter of the soul"—whereas the Impressionists aspired to an emptier gaze—has infused sadness into the scene. But the story of the subject disappears today to the gain of the enchant-

4

4 Edouard Manet: *Luncheon on the Grass*. 1863. Oil on canvas, 214 x 270 cm. Paris, The Louvre

5 Marc-Antoine Raimondi: *The Judgment of Paris*. Engraving after Raphael (detail). Paris, Bibliothèque nationale

6 Titian: *Concert champêtre*. c. 1510-1511 Oil on canvas, 105 x 136.5 cm. Paris, The Rustic Concert. The Louvre (formerly attributed to Giorgione)

Since composition was not his strong point, Manet preferred to borrow from Raphael or Titian, hoping thus to disarm criticism. But both the subject and the technique ran counter to contemporary morals and manners. Here, far removed from any mythological excuses for nudity, is a realistically naked woman, not an artistically undressed one.

7 Auguste-Barthélemy Glaize: *The Country Picnic*. 1850. Oil on canvas, 145 x 114 cm. Montpellier, Musée Fabre

An academician's picnic could be attended by angels . . .

ing color. The partition of tone, for example, is the origin of many of the consequent systematic discoveries of the Impressionists.

There was one discovery besides that of Chevreul that excited the artists, making it henceforth impossible to paint as formerly: photography. "Who among us would be capable of such fidelity, such steadiness in the interpretation of line, such delicacy in the reproduction! Photography is so beautiful . . . it is so beautiful, but one shouldn't admit it!" This remark was from Ingres to one of his pupils. It reflects the uneasiness of the artist before this new art. For artists were at times very afraid of photography, as the cinema was recently afraid of television and the press of audiovisuals. Later, adding the finishing touches to the autochrome, the industrial result of a simultaneous discovery by Ducos de Hauron and Charles Cros in 1869 (a three-color synthesis, a process of fusing into one image the three different proofs obtained by yellow, red, and

8

8   Autochrome Lumière: *Woman with a sunshade in the garden*. c. 1904. Lyons, Fondation Nationale de la Photographie

9   Claude Monet: *Women in the Garden*. 1866–1867. Oil on canvas, 255 x 205 cm. Paris, Musée d'Orsay, Galerie du Jeu de Paume

With this picture Monet meant to prove that he was not only a landscape artist—considered a minor art form, and one that did not bring any medals—but also a figure-painter.

9

blue filters) the Lumière brothers put color at the disposal of photographers. Then, in a fitting turn of events, was to be seen a blossoming of red umbrellas (ill. 11), thanks to the Pointillist texture of potato starch (base of the process), held by all the ladies photographed in a country setting, as a sort of homage to Impressionism.

The Impressionist palette lightened and its forms were broken up. Light pulverized mass. Trees became a single indistinct and shifting blob and shadow acted as punctuation. Landscape became the most important genre, and people became part of the landscape. True creators, they asserted a new vision of the world. They established phenomena which obliged them to paint in a new manner, to invent a way of expressing themselves, for what they had to say did not resemble anything that had gone before. The example of Renoir, in this regard, is significant in the evolution of painting. In the beginning, in his most

11

10   Claude Monet: *Woman with a Sunshade Turned to the Right—Suzanne Hoshedé, daughter of the artist's second wife.* 1866. **Oil on canvas, 131 x 88 cm. Paris, The Louvre**

11   **Autochrome Lumière:** *Woman with Red Sunshade by the Water.* **c. 1904. Lyons, Fondation Nationale de la Photographie**

Autochromes—140 million grains of potato starch under 5000 kilograms of pressure per square centimeter for a plate 13 x 8—were produced in great quantities; for example, 18 million in 1893 alone.

10

12 Berthe Morisot: *The Butterfly Chase*. 1873. Oil on canvas, 46 x 56 cm. Paris, Musée d'Orsay, Galerie du Jeu de Paume

13 Edouard Manet: *Springtime— Jeanne de Marsy*. 1881. Oil on canvas, 73 x 51 cm. New York, Private collection

Manet finally conquered the Salon and received the medal of the Légion d'honneur. His talent was at its highest point. Berthe Morisot married Manet's brother Eugène. The influence of Corot early in her career was soon replaced by that of Manet, though she in turn also influenced him, particularly in persuading him to take up *plein-air* painting

Impressionist period, as in *Madame Choquet Reading* (ill. 16) or *Summer* (ill. 17), the title of which is a good indication of where the artist's quest was taking him, the figure melts into the vagueness of an undefined reality. The third dimension is abolished. The young women do not come forward from the composition in the classical manner. In the middle distance, the flowers are somewhat blurred, obeying the photographic law which does not allow different distances to be simultaneously in focus, and thus the scenery and the model blend into the same light—that of summer. So Renoir, like his friends, replaced the conventions of the studio by lessons of actual experience, fusing science and freedom in a discordant blend.

Renoir began to question his freedom. The spirit of the system might be dangerous, he said to himself. In doubt, a return to the classical tradition could only be beneficial. A trip to Italy allowed him to visit Venice, Rome, the Raphael frescoes at the Villa Farnese, and to go as far as Naples, where he became ecstatic over the Pompeian paintings. "Then there was a break in my work," he would say, "I was at the end of Impressionism and I found that I didn't know how to paint or draw. I was at an impasse." In a period which has been called Ingresesque and which he more correctly called his "sharp style," he stopped suggesting forms by touches of color and outlined them with a firm, clear line, polishing them with a smoother, more pearly finish. But this period which left us such masterpieces as *Dance in the City* (ill. 78) and *Dance in the Country* (ill. 77) lasted only a short time. In quest of his freedom, Renoir came nearer and nearer to Boucher, whom he had always admired. He didn't want to

14

14 Camille Pissarro: *Young Girl with a Stick*. 1881. Oil on canvas, 81 x 64 cm. Paris, The Louvre

In this painting the landscape background is like a tapestry. Pissarro liked

hear any more about Impressionism, but rather about tradition. His young women themselves became landscapes. With the charm and naturalness which are his own he began similarly to evoke them in ripe ears of corn or fruit matured under a summer sun. His personality invaded the canvas. With *Woman in a Straw Hat* (ill. 18) he attained the living image of a moment's happiness. This he wanted to make his chief artistic preoccupation. However, he kept the shimmering luminous strokes of Impressionism, and took from his classical period the lush flesh and the diaphanous robes in a play of pearly transparencies. At the end of his life he alternated bunches of roses with the sinuous and ample body of Venus. Landscapes totally disappeared. They were replaced by roses, which became something of an obsession. When Vollard expressed his astonishment, Renoir replied that they came from his investigation of flesh tones made for his nudes. With *Gabrielle with a Rose* (ill. 19), the final stage of his evolution, he seems to revive, under the Provençal sky which so resembles that of Greece, the ancient myths of the Golden Age. He brings to

to paint women and girls at work in the fields, but his figures are closer to Degas' dancers and working girls than to Millet's gleaners.

the laundresses of Cagnes, to his beloved servant Gabrielle, the grace and nobility of the divinities of Olympus, and he wrote, "How admirable are the Greeks! Their life was so happy that they imagined that in order to find love and paradise the gods had to descend to earth. Yes, earth was the paradise of the gods . . . That's what I want to paint!"

15 Claude Monet. *Evening on the Meadow.* Giverny, 1888. Oil on canvas, 82 x 81 cm. Private collection

19

16 Pierre-Auguste Renoir: *Madame Choquet Reading.* **1876. Oil on canvas, 65.5 by 55 cm. Private collection.**

17 Pierre-Auguste Renoir: *Summer.* **1875. Oil on canvas, 65 x 54 cm. Private collection**

18 Pierre-Auguste Renoir: *Woman in a Straw Hat.* **1884. Oil on canvas, 65.5 x 55.5 cm. Private collection**

19 Pierre-Auguste Renoir: *Gabrielle with a Rose.* **1911. Oil on canvas, 55.5 x 47 cm. Paris, Musée d'Orsay, Galerie du Jeu de Paume**

Renoir's whole career can be seen in these four pictures: his Impressionist period with *Mme. Choquet Reading* and *Summer*, when the model and the background seem to melt into one another. *The Woman in a Straw Hat* exemplifies his post-Ingresque period, with the model dominating the canvas. *Gabrielle* is from the last period, with the model now occupying the entire canvas, the rose echoing the rosy flesh tones which Renoir now painted with his brush tied to his hands, so deformed were they by rheumatism.

Gauguin went to find his paradise in Tahiti (ill. 22). Leaving Brittany and Impressionism at the same time, he departed for the land of dreams. In Brittany, like his Impressionist friends, he at first wanted to affirm his independence, his break with the bourgeoisie, his desire to recover in a simple and natural setting those elementary truths through which the artist can let whatever he feels blossom and find the most suitable means of expression for himself. His technique is therefore that of Impressionism (ill. 20), but he already wanted to escape from a revolution which was not his own, for the first and hardest battles were over when he joined it. He decided to accept the break

21

and to try his chances away from the civilized world. There he introduced into his technique his own means, and began to cultivate more systematically certain procedures such as the use of color, not only in little, glittering, juxtaposed strokes as the Impressionists had done, but also in long parallel hatching, like van Gogh. The most important thing is the appearance of a line around the forms, which is totally opposite to the ideas of Impressionism (ill. 21). His palette became modified, simplified, and adopted warmer and harsher tones in contrast. It was the first step in the transcribing of feeling.

22 Paul Gauguin: *Women of Tahiti*, **or** *On the Beach*. **1891. Oil on canvas, 69 x 91 cm. Paris, Musée d'Orsay, Galerie du Jeu de Paume**

Here Gauguin has become Gauguin. His work now has a tranquil nobility. There is a direct communion between human beings and Nature. Out of this simple grandeur comes a certain mystery, a feeling of pagan religiosity.

II The superior genre

"Each minute costs me one hundred francs," Bouguereau remarked at the peak of his glory to the young Othon Friesz. Meissonnier built himself a sumptuous Neo-Renaissance palace in the Place Malsherbes, thanks to the astronomical sums for which he sold his historical pictures, which were exact down to the last copper button. Léon Bonnet owned a superb art collection which is today at the Bayonne Museum. Academic painting earned a good profit. Vernet, Gérôme, Cabanel, Carolus-Duran were all swimming in opulence. It was the incredible success of Couture's *The Romans of the Decadence* (ill. 40) at the Salon of 1847 which caused Manet's parents to stop opposing their son's career as a painter and to permit him to become a pupil of Couture, sure as they were of his brilliant future under the tutelage of such a master!

This papier-mâché Hollywood was the cause of considerable expenditure on the part of the nouveau riche. The possession of one of these works considerably enhanced the prestige of its owner. The execution of one of these huge pieces of absurdity required months of slave labor because each detail had to be verified, each uniform absolutely authentic. And the shrewd print dealers made fortunes just in selling engravings of the most popular works.

People were as crazy about those pictures then as they are now about a new Godard film. A painter chosen by the Salon had his career assured. A gold medal was worth 4,000 francs while a medal of the second class commanded 1,500. The prizes awarded by the jury established the current value of the artists. A rejected work was unsalable, while a chosen work could be sold for three times the price.

"The Salon is the real battlefield. It's there one must cross swords," declared Manet. Monet, rejected, wrote in 1869, "This fatal rejection almost takes the bread out of my mouth, and despite my modest prices, dealers and collectors turn their backs on me. Above all, it's heartbreaking to see how little interest is taken in a work that isn't a favorite."

We know now that Manet had sought official recognition and the goodwill of the Salons. He did not hesitate to borrow happily from Carrache, Titian, or Goya. He copied Velasquez's *Little Cavalier* from the Louvre, and stayed six long years with Couture. Monet, together with Bazille, Renoir, and Sisley, was a pupil of Gleyre. Degas also began to exhibit at the Salon before joining the Impressionists. At the Louvre he made copies of Giotto, Uccello, Luca Signorelli, and wrote, "Ah, Giotto, let me see Paris, and you, Paris, let me see Giotto." At the same time as he was painting hunting and racing scenes, he undertook a series of five paintings on historical subjects, the famous superior genre, in which he seemed to want to render homage to those painters he admired. The titles of the works speak eloquently: *Young Spartan Girls Inciting Boys to Fight, Semiramis Building Babylon, Alexander and Bucephalus, Jephtha's Daughter*, and finally *Scenes of War from the Middle Ages, or the Misfortunes of Orléans*. He wrote at this time, "I know nothing of inspiration, spontaneity, or temperament; what I do is the result of study and consideration of the great masters . . ."

We should not forget that the Revolution of 1789, followed by the reign of Napoleon, had left many traces. David had gone from *Tennis Court Oath* and the *Death of Marat* to the *Coronation of the Emperor* and the *Distribution of the Eagles*. Overlooking the breath of Romanticism which had already appeared in some of his pictures, and while he still kept the great technical skill which Gombrich calls "the mistake of doing something too well," Meissonnier—"the giant of the dwarfs" according to Degas—showed the extraordinary minutiae of

his execution to general admiration. One could examine his pictures with a magnifying glass; he never forgot the tiniest detail, the least hair of a moustache.

Delacroix was the first to question this heroic style of art, inspired by ancient Greece, and promoted by David and Ingres. Under the force of this shock, academic painting began to vacillate, making possible the great Impressionist revolution. Delacroix retained his preoccupation with decoration and narration, but he dared to apply them to the reality in which he was ideologically caught up: the independence of Greece and the revolt of the Parisian people. Nourished

24

24 Edouard Manet: *The Execution of the Emperor Maximilian.* 1867. Oil on canvas, 196 x 259.8 cm. Boston, Museum of Fine Arts (Gift of Mr. & Mrs. Frank Gair Macomber, 1930)

on Dante, Shakespeare, Le Tasse, Goethe, Scott, and Byron, he succeeded in giving sensual dimensions to the universal myths of the poets. His *Liberty Leading the People* (ill. 25) is the first political composition of modern painting. It marks the moment when the Romantic movement abandoned classical sources for their inspiration and took a decided role in contemporary life. Delacroix wrote to his father, the General, "I have undertaken a modern subject, a barricade . . . even if I can't conquer for my country I can at least paint for her." Here is the voice that would later make the fortune of Déroulède. We can see, in the young drummer boy brandishing a pistol, the model of the Parisian street urchin of *Les Misérables*, created thirty years later by Victor Hugo. Louis-Philippe acquired the picture for 3,000 francs, but took care not to exhibit it.

In 1857 Manet paid a visit to Delacroix to ask his permission to copy *Dante and Virgil in Hell* at the National Museum. He only wanted to do it in the superior genre transposed to the modern epoch, but once again his avant-garde technique betrayed his intentions. Whether it was a question of *The Trumpet* (ill. 23), or the celebrated *Fife Player*, which had been rejected by the Salon jury, he carved out a silhouette which Daumier, who admired him, said had all the freshness and daring of a playing card. It is, in effect, up to the viewer to reconstitute the mass from what Manet offers him, and this relation between the work of art and the effort of the eye which looks at it is the basis, not only of Impressionism, but also of all modern art. Obviously, at the time, people laughed. *The Execution of the Emperor Maximilian* (ill. 24) has for its subject a contemporary political event of such burning immediacy that Manet finally gave up trying to depict it. Goya's *Third of May* minus what the picture signifies, represents, according to Malraux, what modern painting could be if

25

26

25 Eugène Delacroix: *Liberty Leading the People, 28 July 1830.* 1830. **Oil on canvas, 259 x 325 cm. Paris, The Louvre**

26 Ernest Meissonnier: *The Siege of Paris.* 1870. **Oil on canvas, 53 x 70 cm. Paris, The Louvre**

Goya, Delacroix and Manet all took a position on contemporary events. After such pictures, the art of the 19th century had to change, abandoning antiquity for its inspiration and taking up instead the history of its own time.

27   Ernest Meissonier: *The Campaign in France, 1814.* 1861. Oil on canvas, 51 x 76 cm. Paris, The Louvre

28   *Napoléon III at the Battle of Magenta, 8 June 1859.* Lithograph. Paris, Bibliothèque nationale

29   Adolphe Yvon. *The Annexation of the Suburbs, 16 June 1859, Napoléon III Delivers the Annexation Decree to Haussmann.* 1860. Oil on canvas, 140 x 102 cm. Paris, Bibliothèque historique de la Ville

30   *The Empress Shooting in Marly.* Engraving. Paris, Bibliothèque nationale.

31   Darjou: *The Empress Eugénie in Egypt in 1869 for the Inauguration of the Suez Canal.* Drawing which appeared in *Le Monde illustré*

Never had France been divided into two such violently opposing camps. The Emperor paraded on horseback, The Empress went shooting and set the fashions. Women's dresses were overloaded with lace, flounces, ribbons and artificial flowers. A canal was dug in Egypt, Mexico was colonized. Paris got a face-lift from Baron Haussmann which pushed an invasive and dangerous proletariat into the outskirts.

32

33

32 Edouard Follet: *Marriage of Napoleon III and the Empress Eugénie (January 8, 1853)*. **Engraving after Henri Felix Emmanuel Philippoteaux. Paris, Bibliothèque nationale**

33 *Empress Eugénie's Wedding Dress.* **Fashion drawing in** *Le Conseiller des Dames et des Demoiselles,* **January 1853**

34 *Napoleon III Receiving Rulers and Illustrious Personages who Visited the Universal Exposition of 1867.* **Lithograph. Paris, Bibliothèque nationale, Print Room**

The Emperor annexed Cochin China in 1856, the results of which would have consequences well past his century. An alliance with Great Britain and Turkey to invade the Crimea resulted in the enmity of the Tsar. The subsequent war with Germany, after he had alienated both Britain and Italy, resulted in his defeat. The Paris Commune followed, with barricades and summary execution. Accused of having helped pull down the Column in the Place Vendôme, Courbet had to flee to Switzerland.

34

removed from all meaning other than the art of painting. The simultaneousness of the sensations prevails over the compositional hierarchy. Certain figures have a disproportionate scale, the colored masses abound. What counts is only the effect of the whole. In front of *The Cavaliers* at the Louvre, then attributed to Velasquez, and which he was copying, Manet had had a revelation. "Ah, it's clear and distinct! That's why you're so disgusted with all these stews and sauces."

Baudelaire had said: the true painter will know how to extract the epic side of real life and understand how great and poetic we are in our ties and our varnished boots." With *Music in the Tuileries*, Manet was the first to discover the new spectacle of his city and its time, the poetry of modern life. That was the "modernity" demanded by the author of the *Fleurs du mal*, a modernity that created an immediate scandal. Poor Manet, he was only looking for that freedom of touch that certain old masters had had—the Venetians, Franz Hals, Rembrandt, Velasquez—without realizing that under Napoleon III that freedom was no longer in vogue; much preferred was the gloomy and formal solemnity of "great painting" in the manner of Bouguereau. Daring composition and color made the public uneasy about innovation. How daring to show for the first time the bourgeois Parisians in their Sunday best, crowded together and devoting themselves to the ritual of conversation and politely raised hats! (Today, it would be a big August holiday at the seaside.) Through Manet, we see for the first time a general view of a society whose everyday appearance is translated by a pure fancy. As in the *Maximilian*, the subject is transcended. What one retains above all is the animated repetition of the cylindrical shapes of tall hats, grouped around the blooming flowers of the women's hats, coiffures, and feminine clothing painted in clear, flat tints heightened with a few sharp notes of brilliant color.

After such a picture, Monet, Renoir, and their friends were able to set off the firework of Impressionism and let it take its course. Why, really, did young ambitious artists like the Impressionists become rebels, contestants, and spoilsports, sometimes despite themselves? Because sincerity had never gone hand in hand with the commercial organization of art. Their honest approach to what they painted was an insurmountable barrier that separated them from the taste of their time. "Being unable to throw myself into a large composition," said Bazille, "I have tried to paint my best on the simplest possible subject; in any case I think the subject matters little, provided I can make it interesting from the painter's point of view." These painters were not only obsessed by light, they were also obsessed by painting. Vainly, like Manet, they surrounded themselves with the best references, sought the elements of landscape in Rubens and Carrache, seeking only to reach the superior genre; but at the moment of attainment, without even realizing it, they were thrown into disorder, and something else appeared from their brush. In short, they refused to prostitute themselves to official taste, and they automatically chose freedom. Degas, surely the most intelligent and subtle of them, summed up the phenomenon in two phrases: "One sees as one wants to see, and this falsity makes art." And: "We must bewitch truth, giving it the appearance of mania." And Courbet, who wished to "degrade" art, said, "I have crossed tradition as a good swimmer would cross a river; the academicians have drowned in it." Van Gogh, the most mystical, said in his turn: "In my life and painting I can do without the good God. But I can never, as I suffer here, do without something which is greater than I, than my life itself: the power of creation."

What reigned in opposition to them was the triumphant bourgeoisie of which Jarry's Ubu-Roi was the ideal: "To eat sausage frequently and keep a carriage." "The bourgeois," wrote Huysmans in *Against the Grain*, "reassured, lords it jovially by force of his money and the contagion of his stupidity. The result of his advent was the eradication of all intelligence, the negation of integrity, and the death of art." When the Impressionists hurled themselves into the arena, Monsieur Prudhomme reigned. He was, according to Zola, the contemporary Maecenas. He was the State and the soul of the official juries. It was a sort of cold war, where anything was allowed. These artists, like Cézanne, wanted "to make of Impressionism something as solid and lasting as the art in the museums."

35

36

35 *The Paris Commune Pulling Down the Vendôme Column.* **Popular engraving. Paris, Bibliothèque nationale**

36 *Place Vendôme, the National Guard with an Assault Vehicle.* **Anonymous photograph. Paris, Bibliothèque nationale**

37 **Edouard Manet:** *Music in the Tuileries.* **1862. Oil on canvas, 76 x 119 cm. London, National Gallery** ▷

"As Levin, thanks to the Russian proletariat, drew from the ruins of capitalism the shape of a new world, Cézanne drew from the ruins of academic painting not only modern art, but the revival of forms five thousand years old," noted Malraux, with that well-known economy displayed in *The Paths of Silence*.

Even when the Impressionist adventure came to an end, the battle continued. When Monet said in 1883 to Durand-Ruel, "I am less and less satisfied with myself," and Renoir, being "almost at his end," leaving as a testament that sublime piece of nonsense, *The Boating Party*, admitted in the same year,

39 Paul Gauguin: *Joseph and Potiphar's wife.* **1896. Oil on canvas. 89 x 116 cm. Private collection**

Two ways of approaching the "Superior Genre"; in a Tahitian decor with Gauguin and his *Potiphar's Wife,* who looks like the vahine who shared his hut in Papeete; or in a cardboard decor with the academician Couture, primarily known for having been Manet's teacher.

"There has been a break in my work"; when Degas and Pissarro also experienced the effects of that crisis and were uneasy, one canvas, relegated to the refreshment room of the Exhibition of Independent Artists of 1884 because of its huge size, would try to resolve the problems of the Impressionists. It was the *Bathers at Asnières* by Seurat.

"This picture," says Paul Signac, "being painted in large flat strokes, balanced against each other and coming from a palette made up of clear and earthy colors, like that of Delacroix, seems dulled because of the ochre and earth shades, less brilliant than those painted by the Impressionists with their palette of prismatic colors. But the observation of the laws of contrast, the methodical separation of elements—light, shadow, local color, reaction—their just proportion and their balance confer a perfect harmony upon the painting."

The climate of the times was completely steeped in positivism. People believed in money, but also in science. Seurat wanted to overcome the instantaneous, ephemeral perception in order to make the transitory eternal by making use of this knowledge, which penetrated all realms of literature and philosophy. He was sure that there existed a science of art whose laws he could discover, in optics and the chemistry of color as well as in the work of the masters he admired. What interested him most about Delacroix, as he said himself, was "the strictest application of scientific precepts seen through a personality." He familiarized himself with Maxwell's experiments with polychrome discs, and with many other discoveries, each with a more barbarous name than the one before: the dichrooscope of Dove, an apparatus which mixed the light coming from colored glass; the shistoscope of Brücke, which produced complementary colors. He understood the theory of Helmholtz on the sensibility of the eye. He made the acquaintance of Charles Henry, librarian at the Sorbonne, inventor, man of erudition, and author of an *Introduction to the Scientific Aesthetic*, whose object was to reduce Degas' pictures to equations.

The miracle is that all this science, often shoddy, didn't succeed in holding back either the charm or power of Seurat's work. He said to Charles Augrand, "They want to find poetry in what I do. No, I just use my method, that's all." The Impressionists had liberated the role of color, to the detriment of form. Seurat developed the principle of the little stroke to inaugurate the system of Pointillism. But if the Impressionist stroke has a purely analytical aim, the dot is essentially constructive and compositional. Seurat took up the open-air scenes that were so dear to his elders, but he raised them to a monumental level, to the "superior genre" of Piero della Francesca's frescoes at Arezzo, of which he had seen copies at the School of Fine Arts. In these large compositions, the illusion of perspective and the atmospheric vibrations of his predecessors are attenuated to give place to a kind of crystallization, of solidification destined to defy time. Certainly, it is possible to make fun of these "Confettisms," "Pointillisms," and other "Blobisms," but the essential thing about the technique is not the dot, but the splitting of color tone. Signac adopted the term "Divisionism," and Félix Fénéon invented the name "Neo-Impressionism," but Seurat, while allowing him the use of the latter word, preferred to call it "Luminism": the art of painting with the colors of light and using pigments in their pure state. Luminism had a considerable influence on numerous avant-garde artists of the twentieth century. From the Fauves to the Cubists and Futurists, from the suprematism of Malévitch to the Neo-Plasticism of Mondrian and the experiments of the Surrealists. They all owed something to Seurat.

That "Sunday Impressionist" Gauguin would also continue the fight in his own way. From "commas" to "hatching" he was to arrive at the "arabesque," the "synthesis," and the "constant," the watchwords of his most ambitious works.

40 Thomas Couture: *The Romans of the Decadence.* 1847. Oil on canvas, 466 x 775 cm. Paris, The Louvre

Hadn't he realized the secret wishes of most of his friends, to sever relations with oppressive daily life, break off from family and western civilization, and discover a lost freshness? His choice of Tahiti—for good reason called "the new Cytheria" by Bougainville—was not accidental. Gauguin had already begun painting Tahitian women in Brittany. Above all, his ambition was not bound by the curves of his models and the search for new harmonies; he was also haunted by the "superior genre." He too wanted to paint those enormous irrelevances that would achieve the synthesis of form and color, as opposed to the Impressionist analysis. He took with him and fastened to the walls of his hut reproductions of works which he held dear, Egyptian frescoes, bas reliefs from the

Javanese temple of Borobudur, and Japanese prints (ill. 42-44). And the long-awaited miracle occurred. Even though he had recourse to the structural schema borrowed from the art and culture of the whole world—European, Japanese, Egyptian (*Ta Matete*, ill. 41, is just like an Egyptian fresco)—Gauguin's art attained simplicity and effectiveness thanks to the luxuriance of the colors offered by the landscape, and the dominant curves, as much of the body as of nature. "Everything blinds me, dazzles me, in this landscape," he was to avow. But above all, as Françoise Cachin wrote, "The hermit of Pouldu devoted his poetic energies to the Tahitians. Right from the beginning, with an unerring touch, he established for eternity their kind of beauty."

41 Paul Gauguin: *Ta Matete (The Market)*. 1892. Oil on canvas, 73 x 92 cm. Basel, Kunstmuseum

42-44 Photographs of Egyptian frescoes, reliefs of the Javanese temple of Borobudur, and a Japanese print, all found in Gauguin's hut at Tahiti and bought by Victor Segalen at the auction sale of September 1903. France, collection of Mme. Joly-Segalen

Popular legend has it that only crass ignorance could explain the insane approach to painting of the "blob" school. Manet went to the Louvre to copy Tintoretto and Titian and met Degas copying Velasquez. Cézanne spent much time before Veronese, Poussin and Chardin. Renoir took inspiration from the *Marriage at Cana* for his *Luncheon of the Boating Party*. It was said of him that he repainted Courbet with Delacroix's palette. Gauguin was inspired by Greek statues for his most exotic pictures, and lived surrounded by Japanese prints and photographs of Egyptian frescoes or Javanese reliefs pinned on the walls. In *Ta Matete* he borrowed from the Egyptian frescoes.

45

III   The spleen of Paris

In order to realize an old dream of the kings of France, the reuniting of the Louvre with the Tuileries, Napoleon III ordered in 1854 the destruction of the houses that cluttered the courtyards of the Louvre and the Carrousel. This also entailed removing an encroaching and combative proletariat spawned by runaway industrialization. Napoleon had become Emperor of the French three years earlier by a coup d'état, which had occasioned the death of more than two hundred workers on the barricades. In 1869 there were still bleeding wounds. We should remember that the First International was in 1864. A work had appeared in 1848 that opened with the famous phrase: "A spectre haunts Europe: the spectre of Communism" and ended with the call: "Workers of the world, unite!" The Communist Party Manifesto, issued by Marx and Engels.

In Paris, which sheltered two million inhabitants, there were, at the end of the Empire, five hundred thousand workers, of whom a hundred and twelve thousand were women. They earned two francs a day for thirteen hours of work, six hundred francs a year. Now, an attic cost a hundred and twenty francs a year rent. The renovation of Paris by Baron Haussmann, from the great boulevards to les Halles—that "belly of Paris," according to Zola—including the new Opéra of Garnier, did not just expand the world's image of Paris as the "City of Light." Apart from the capital's "face-lift," the most noticeable result of the new urbanization was the sharp separation established thereafter between the workers' districts, situated on the periphery, and the middle-class districts. Haussmann's first objective had been to eradicate the hovels which swarmed all over, replacing them by boulevards—one of which bears his name—whose great right-angled arteries could facilitate repression in the case of any popular uprising.

In this Paris, remodeled by Napoleon III to bolster his wavering popularity, the Universal Exposition of 1867 was the last straw. The city had become in Baudelaire's words "a great harlot." From above, in his balloon, Nadar photographed it—dense, orderly, immense, and glittering. In its bosom crawled the crowd, which cohered, became thicker, invaded the sidewalks and the terraces. For the new painters there was a "delight in choosing to live in the crowd, in its eddy and flow, its transience and its boundlessness," wrote Baudelaire, who stated—according to Constantin Guy, witness both for him and for "*the modern*"—that his desire and his business was to "marry the crowd." In his preface to *The Spleen of Paris*, the poet observes that such a passion for the crowd must produce a new language, a poetic prose, "both supple and bruised enough" to reflect the "comings and goings of big cities." It must also produce a new kind of painting: "There is a rapid movement in the life of the people, in the daily metamorphosis of outward things, that demands an equal speed of execution from the artist." With a nervous style of drawing and an execution so flexible that it seems instantaneous, Manet painted with rapid strokes views of Paris that are his most direct contribution to Impressionism, especially of the rue Mosnier, where he had his studio. He painted the view from its window in very luminous, modulated pictures in which the animation of the streets is conveyed by means of small strokes. He had already come a long way from the simplistic teaching he had received at Couture's studio. The Impressionists learned from him, along with so much else, direct observation. From them, in turn, he learned that "shadow is not only realized by turning tones towards black, but that it can be the product of a decomposition of light in a given area and on planes which are only seen and established as cool colors." (R. Rey).

45   Claude Monet: *The rue Montorgueil, Fête, 30 June 1878*. 1878. Oil on canvas, 80 x 150.5 cm. Paris, Musée d'Orsay,

The Impressionists discovered the "modernity" of the city. But it soon became an excuse for them to display their virtuosity. It is necessary to step back and see how all those little bits of color, quite abstract when seen close up, become transformed into flags and the movement of the crowd. Here Monet offers one of the first examples of a perspective view—à la Hiroshige—shown from high up, as Pissarro, Renoir or Caillebotte, all great collectors of Japanese prints, would enjoy doing.

46 Camille Pissarro: *Boulevard Montmartre, Night Effect*. 1897. Oil on canvas, 54 x 65 cm. London, National Gallery

Pissarro was a sort of father to the Impressionists, being about ten years older. Together with Monet he would stay faithful to Impressionism all his life. Towards its end, having endured both loneliness and poverty, but always a master, though with failing eyesight, he executed a series of views of Paris. This night scene of the Boulevard Montmartre, the only one he ever did, is the culmination of an art which involved the spectator. A few strokes are sufficient to evoke a gas lamp, a cab, or a swarming crowd. He used economy of means, because he knew that the brain and the eye of the viewer would supply the rest.

It is interesting to compare these airy works in frontal perspective and with little depth with the comparable attempt of Monet to paint the rue Montorgueil, decked with flags, on the occasion of the Universal Exposition of 1878. That work is presented as a barrage of impressions, with the composition based on swirling diagonals, the red of the flags punctuating the facades with their elongated windows, and the swarming crowds translated into a dominant green. With this important picture, we see that Monet is no longer dominated by the urge to bear witness to his time, but is rather haunted by the pictorial problems of reproducing the scene by those flat strokes which he has made his means of expression. "It's not the subject that creates the picture, but rather the painting that creates the subject," notes Jean Clay. The flags, those little squares of pure color, constitute the ideal subject. Monet's use of them allows him to give a feeling of perspective while retaining their monochromatic value. The theme was to be taken up again in almost the same way by Van Gogh and subsequently by the Fauves. They will radicalize the set purposes of *The rue Montorgueil* and keep only its play of color.

In 1866, Monet eagerly went up onto the roofs of the Louvre, opposite Sainte-Germain-l'Auxerrois, to paint the first panoramic views of Paris. These paintings offer many depictions of the quais and the place Dauphine, sometimes brilliant with light, sometimes bathed in luminous shadow, dominated by the cupolas of the Pantheon, by the Val-de-Grâce, and by the Tour Clovis, which stands out under the wide dappled skies. The masses of greenery or the groves of light foliage create an extensive, transparent space. The animated silhouettes of cabs and pedestrians stand out in the foreground. These are the first urban landscapes, these panoramic and dizzying views of the boulevards and of the Pont Neuf, which would continue to inspire his friends until the end of the century. Some will even go as far as to collaborate and divide up the work, like Pissarro and Cézanne in *The Hermitage at Pontoise* (ill. 49), in which Cézanne did the landscape and left the figures to Pissarro, who was more adroit with them.

Faced with the city, the Impressionists behave in the same way as they do with the countryside: they reject the illusion of line and seek only to capture the vibrations. One critic will speak of the "innumerable thin black strokes in the lower part of the picture" that represent the passers-by. But another will understand their work better: "Never has the prodigious animation of the highways, the crowd swarming on the asphalt and the carriages on the streets, the tossing of the trees of the boulevard in the dust and light, always elusive, fleeting, instantaneous, never have they been thus caught and fixed in their extraordinary fluidity." To avoid setting up their easels in the middle of a crowd, the Impressionists often painted, as Manet did, from a window. This resulted in a swooping view, which changed the focus and gave a foreshortening effect that prefigures the motion picture camera. Because of that, the viewer no longer observes the subject from a distance but has the impression of being directly involved in the life of the city.

There is nothing like a good war for providing a salutary break in one's routine. The Impressionists were individualists. With the news of the declaration of war on Prussia, each reacted in his own way. Bazille enlisted immediately and died no less quickly. On the 28th of November he fell in battle at Beaune-la-Rolande, leaving only the suggestion of what might have been

47 Camille Pissarro: *Le Pavillon de Flore and the Pont Royal.* **1903. Oil on canvas, 65.5 x 81 cm. Private collection**

47

48 Pierre-August Renoir: *The Champs-Elysées, During the Exposition universelle of 1867*. **1867. Oil on canvas, 76.5 x 130.2 cm. Zurich, Private collection**

achieved. Cézanne, on the contrary, a little concerned at being on the roster for military service, left Aix-en-Provence and the peace of the family for work at l'Estaque. Renoir was taken into a regiment of cuirassiers, first at Bordeaux and then at Tarbes. Degas at the coast and Manet at Le Havre both left hastily for Paris. They would await the fall of the Empire before the first would join

the artillery and the second, the National Guard. Monet succeeded in reaching England, where Pissarro was soon to join him.

Ever since the Romantic era there had been numerous and fruitful literary and artistic exchanges between England and France. Géricault and Delacroix had had contact with Bonington and the Fieldings. Whistler, dividing his life

Here Renoir's colors are still close to reality, but following a meeting in the woods with Diaz, painter of the Barbizon school, his palette has lightened. The shapes are beginning to break up, like Sisley, the trees are a single stroke, and the shadows act like punctuation, in the manner of Manet. Renoir is ready to absorb the influence of Monet and their double view of La Grenouillère will see the true birth of Impressionism.

49   Paul Cézanne/Camille Pissarro: *The Hermitage at Pontoise.* 1873. Oil on canvas, 55 x 46 cm. Paris, Private collection

Cézanne was a good landscape artist; Pissarro was better at figures. This is an unusual example of the intelligent division of labor—Cézanne and his master Pissarro amused themselves by working on the same canvas.

between London and Paris, had formed and maintained a sort of bridge between two worlds of art, which were becoming more and more divergent. For Monet and Pissarro, at an identical stage of development, the enforced stay of 1870-71 seemed a happy intervention of destiny on the triple planes of influence, confirmation, and encounters. "In London they studied his work (Turner) and analyzed his technique. At first they were bowled over by his effects of snow and ice. They were astonished at the way in which he succeeded in suggesting the whiteness of the snow, they who, until now, had not been successful with their large white brushstrokes. They concluded that this marvellous result was not obtained by a uniform whiteness, but by a great number of dots of different color, set side by side and producing the desired effect from a distance." (Signac, *De Delacroix au Néo-Impressionisme*).

Pissarro for his part wrote in a letter to Dewhurst in November 1902, "In 1870 I found myself with Monet in London and we met Daubigny and Bonvin; Monet and I were enthusiastic about the London landscapes. Monet worked in the parks while I, living at that time in Lower Norwood, a charming suburb, studied the effects of fog, snow, and springtime. We worked from nature, and later Monet painted several superb studies of fog in London. Equally as often we went to museums. The watercolors and paintings of Turner and Constable, as well as the canvases of 'Old Crome' certainly influenced us. We admired Gainsborough, Lawrence, and Reynolds, but above all we were astounded by the landscape artists who were closest to our own seeking for affinity with the

49

open air, with light, and with transitory effects." Thus Monet and Pissarro, thanks to the war, found in London, in the work of Turner and Constable, the confirmation of their own undertaking, now in full development. However, one must put things in their proper place. Pissarro also declared to Dewhurst, as an example of the profoundly scrupulous and exacting spirit of an artist: "Turner and Constable were useful to us, as all great painting has been. But the basis of our art is indisputably French by tradition. Our masters are Clouet, Nicolas Poussin, Claude Lorrain, the eighteenth century with Chardin and the 1830 group with Corot." It is true that Impressionism had to evolve well beyond the Romanticism of Turner.

We might also add that in regard to a view such as *Parliament, London* (ill. 52), the American critic William Seitz could speak of the "latent romanticism" of Monet: "Here he accentuates the mysterious effect of atmosphere not only by extreme simplification, but by notable limitation and by raising the towers and gothic spires." In order to paint the Houses of Parliament, the artist stationed himself at a window, surrounded by several canvases in various stages from among which he selected the one which seemed most appropriate to the moment. Thirty-seven views of the Thames were exhibited in 1904, at Galerie Durand-Ruel.

The war and the trip to London had another happy consequence. They allowed the Impressionists to become acquainted with the dealer Durand-Ruel who had left Paris with his pictures and had just opened a gallery in New Bond

50 Vincent van Gogh: *The Restaurant of la Sirène at Asnières.* 1887. Oil on canvas, 57 x 68 cm. Paris, Musée d'Orsay

Newly arrived in the capital, where he met the Impressionists and their color, Van Gogh underwent a new experience. He went for long walks to Asnières, Joinville, Suresnes, Chatou, and little by little his palette lightened and the pointillist dots appeared. Perhaps it was the light of Paris, rather than that of the south, which transformed the painter of Dutch peasants.

51   Joseph Mallord William Turner:
The Burning of the Houses of Lords and Commons, 16 October, 1834. 1835. 1855. Oil on canvas, 92 x 123 cm. Philadelphia, Philadelphia Museum of Art (John H. McFadden Collection)

52   Claude Monet: *Parliament, London Sun piercing the Fog.* 1904. Oil on canvas, 81 x 92 cm. Paris, The Louvre.

One of the paradoxes of Impressionism is its double connection of Realism and Romanticism. It borrowed technique from the latter, while rejecting its subjects, but Turner's romantic vision supplanted the precise observation of reality.

53 Claude Monet: *Rouen Cathedral, Portal in Dull Weather.* 1894. Oil on canvas, 100 x 65 cm. Paris, Musée d'Orsay, Galerie du Jeu de Paume

54 Claude Monet: *Rouen Cathedral, Portal and Albane Tower.* 1894. Oil on canvas, 107 x 73 cm. Paris, The Louvre

Street. At that time he was interested in the Barbizon School, but began to consider the Impressionists as possible successors to Corot, Diaz, Daubigny, and Courbet. He was henceforth to play a determining role in the survival and eventual triumph of Impressionism.

Degas intended to study diverse kinds of smoke—that of cigarettes, of chimneys, trains, and ships. Monet's preference was for the formless elements like water, steam, clouds, mist, snow, ice. He blended them, as in the steam and clouds above the trains that are no more than an odd black spot. No Romanticism here, as in Turner. Nor was there a message as Zola's making a modern allegory of *La Bête Humaine.* No social purpose as with the Pointillists who, ten years later, would paint the desolate suburbs and gasworks.

People spoke of the Romanticism of Monet, and accused him, together with Pissarro, of being merely simple disciples of the lyrical Englishman. Doubtless it was for this reason that Monet never missed an opportunity to remark that since before his trip to London in 1870, he had been more realistic and analytical than Turner, adding that the English artist was repugnant to him because of his exuberant Romanticism. However this "Raphael of water" as Manet dubbed him, never liked that element so much as when it became mist or steam. This became the subject of the Gare St.-Lazare paintings, with plumes of steam rising from the train funnels, a motif dear to the heart of Turner, that master of the impalpable.

According to his custom, in 1893 Monet took up residence in a room fronting the cathedral at Rouen. He placed several easels in front of the window, scrutinized the façade of the building, and went from one easel to the next according to the time of day. He made two visits devoted to the study of the successive play of light and shadow on the cathedral. Some fifty canvases resulted (ill. 53, 54). "One cannot say," wrote Malevitch, "that Claude Monet has reflected bourgeois religious ideology in the cathedral at Rouen. That's because he worked above all on the purely physical aspect of the light changing on the façade." And Monet, in turn, explained, "For me the subject is an insignificant thing. What I want to reproduce is what exists between the subject and myself." The enduring effects of the cathedrals are immense; they foretell the celebrated *Painted Façades* of Braque and Picasso fifteen years later. Michel Hoog takes note of this "approach to the abstract." "The cathedral of Rouen . . . obliges whole generations to change their conception of pictorial painting."

55 Claude Monet: *Gare St.-Lazare.* ▷
1877. Oil on canvas, 75.5 x 104 cm.
Paris, Musée d'Orsay, Galerie du Jeu
de Paume

56 James McNeill Whistler: *Old Bat-* ▷
tersea Bridge. 1865. Oil on canvas, 66 x
50 cm. London, Tate Gallery

57 Ando Hiroshige: *Moonlight at Ry-* ▷
ogoku. 1832. Color print, 39 x 25 cm.
New York, The Brooklyn Museum

58 Gustave Caillebotte: *Le Pont de* ▷
l'Europe. 1876. Oil on canvas, 65 x 81
cm. New York, Stephen Hahn Gallery

The Japanese school of Hiroshige, Whistler and Caillebotte was something new. It also exemplified what had been called, since Leonardo da Vinci, atmospheric or aerial perspective, meaning that the further away an object was the more hazy and bluish it should be painted.

IV The tools of labor

In the same way as Balzac or Zola, Degas, who was (like Manet) concerned with interpreting the life of society but who conceived of such interpretation more methodically and systematically, had had the idea of forming a series of contemporary subjects. He laid out for himself an ambitious program, which would permit him to elaborate on a certain number of themes: musicians and their instruments; the bakery with the shapes of breads and cakes; the actions entailed in the practice of a craft, such as the hands of a hairdresser, the movements of a dancer's legs—these he often painted apart from the rest of the body—and the weariness of laundresses.

Aestheticism was not for Courbet, the "strong workman" who was said to have worked "more to be a man than a painter." When he cleared the way for the Impressionists, opening the path for Manet's *Luncheon on the Grass* (ill. 4) with his *Young Women on the Banks of the Seine,* (ill. 2) or with his *Afternoon at Ornans* foreshadowing *The Card Players* (ill. 75) of Cézanne, he was not only a forerunner; he went beyond Impressionism and augured the Constructive Realism of the twentieth century. His purpose was quite different from theirs, and doubtless he would not have cared for the development of their aestheticism or the blurred colors of their palettes. His desire was to bear witness for the humble, the obscure, the peasants, and the workers. Among all the Venuses, the Hercules, the battle scenes and martyrdoms of the academicians, he placed his *Stone Breaker,* (ill. 65) and his celebrated *Funeral at Ornans*: an incursion that was considered in very bad taste. He affirmed, "I am not only a socialist, but a good democrat and republican; in a word, I am a partisan of all revolutions and above all, a realist. By realist I mean that I am a sincere friend of the real truth." But he rejected the label of "Realist," saying, "Titles have never given a correct idea of things; if it were otherwise, works of art would be superfluous . . . in brief, to make living art is my aim." He took from Constable a phrase which he made his slogan, "Nothing in nature is ugly." Together with his friend Proud'hon who had published *On the Principles of Art and its Social Objectives,* and in opposition to the symbolic allegories which flourished in the Salons, Courbet showed what he termed "actual allegories." This was one of his greatest audacities and one which shocked the most, to give to realistic scenes a breath of the epic, a Rembrandt-like atmosphere, and to depict in such grand formats people generally considered insignificant, people who had, up till then, had the right to appear in only the most modest canvasses.

Millet, "a peasant himself" (Delacroix), four years older than Courbet, was content to paint *The Angelus* without wanting to make a manifesto out of it. Nevertheless, the vigor of his art, an eloquent witness to the misery of the time, was not always admired: *The Beaters, The Reapers' Repast,* and even the famous *Sower* (1850) were often proclaimed trivial and coarse. According to Millet, the trivial must be made to express the sublime. *The Gleaners* (ill. 59) aroused unforeseen criticism: "Behind these three gleaners are visible against the leaden horizon foreshadowings of the rioting populace and the scaffolds of '93." One might say that the journalist who wrote those lines in *Le Figaro* was already practicing the same system of poison that is distilled in many of today's dailies by his confrères. Baudelaire was not kind and reproached Millet for his "dark and deadly brutalization" of his heroes, his tendency to preach, and added, "His style will bring him misfortune." Millet's palette, dominated by browns

62 Jules Breton: *The Gleaner.* 1877. Oil on canvas, 230 x 124 cm. Arras, Musée des Beaux-Arts

A peasant girl of powerful aspect proclaims social realism—an Academician in the land of the Soviets.

59 Jean-François Millet: *The Gleaners.* 1857. Oil on canvas, 83.6 x 111 cm. Paris, The Louvre

60 Paul Gauguin: *Peasant Woman of Brittany.* 1889. Oil on canvas, 80.5 x 35.5 cm. Bradford, Collection of Dr. & Mrs. T.E. Hanley

61 Vincent van Gogh: *Noon* or *The Siesta* 1890. 73 x 91 cm. Paris, Musée d'Orsay

Throughout his correspondence with his brother Théo, Van Gogh constantly repeated the words "My master, Millet." He devoted much time to Millet's painting and copied twenty-four black-and-white engravings in oil, improvising the color. He thought that Millet's habit (and later, Monet's) of executing a series of paintings on a single theme at different times of the day made for easier comprehension by the public. He called the elder painter "brother"—a word of great emotional significance for Vincent.

and grays, is also capable of bold harmonies such as the blue and red in *The Gleaners*, and in his very last canvases we sense the rise of what will be Impressionism. When he began to work, Van Gogh's only wish was to follow the man whom he called, in his long correspondence with his brother Théo, "Millet, my master." "Working scenes give me a lot of trouble yet," he wrote, "we should always portray them in such a way that they appear well done beside Dutch painting, both in color and tone." And about *The Potato Eaters*: "In painting that, I thought again of what was so rightly said of Millet's peasants: 'His peasants seem to be painted with the earth they are sowing' ... the heads ... I have painted them without pity or hesitation, and the color I

63

The Impressionists are, above all, painters of color and light. But they also excel at drawing. They filled many notebooks with quick sketches of topographic detail, or movement which they would use later.

have made them now is a little like that of a very earthy potato, unpeeled, naturally." ... As for his refusal to use white, he explained: "I am quite certain that if you had asked Millet, Daubigny, or Corot to paint a snowscape without using white they would have done it, and that the snow would appear white in their pictures."

So these artists from Millet to Gauguin declined to take refuge in the myths of ancient history and showed their heroes at work in the humility and fatigue of their daily tasks and actions (ill. 59-67). This grip of the ideological conscience which from then on constituted the irreplaceable heritage of all modern art, put pressure on the linguistic structure, both modifying and renewing it, and augmenting its communicative effectiveness. In that sense, their lesson is of fundamental importance.

Degas's motivation was quite different. He explained, "They call me the painter of dancers and they don't understand that for me the dancer is an excuse to paint pretty fabrics and to depict movement." Cynically he remarked

G.Courbet

to a rich subscriber at the Opera who wanted to carry off a dancer, "Sir, you have no right to deprive us of our tools!" There was something of both the engineer and the photographer in Degas, in the precision of his analysis and the refinement of his copying. Edmond de Goncourt paid him a visit at the beginning of February 1874. "Yesterday I spent the whole day in the studio of a strange painter by the name of Degas. After much hesitation, tiptoeing—in all senses of the word—he is now enamored of the modern; and here he has fixed

65 Gustave Courbet: *The Stone Breaker*. c. 1865. Black stone heightened with red chalk on cream paper, 31.5 x 23.9 cm. Ornans, Musée Courbet

In 1848 the people had showed their faces for the first time and frightened the bourgeoisie somewhat. It was then considered subversive to depict them. This drawing of Courbet is a preparatory study for *The Stone Breaker*, a picture which ruffled the academic waters and caused the artist to be called in turn, "the Messiah of democratic art," "the first socialist painter," "the people's Velasquez" and "the Raphael of the stone heaps."

66 Paul Gauguin: *Man with an Axe*. 1891. Oil on canvas, 92 x 70 cm. New York, Collection of Mr. & Mrs. Alex M. Lewyt

67 Jean-François Millet: *The Man with a Hoe*. 1862. Drawing, 28.5 x 17 cm. Paris, Collection of Claude Aubry

Although so much at home in the world of the tropics, Gauguin was also influenced by other cultures more distant— Egypt, Java, Japan and Greece. *The Man with an Axe* is directly inspired by a horseman in the Parthenon frieze. Here we have a Greek among the vahines! Gauguin was always an anti-colonial and his natural combativeness opposed what he saw as impediments to the natural expansion of the native people. He even founded a polemical journal, *Le Sourire*, which he wrote, edited, illustrated and produced himself on a mimeograph machine.

66

his choice on laundresses and dancers. He sets them before us, with the most charming foreshortening, laundresses and still more laundresses, speaking their language and explaining to us the techniques of ironing, pressing, etc. Then the dancers come before us . . . the painter shows his pictures, sometimes explaining by mimicry a choreographic development, or imitating one of the dancer's arabesques. It is really very amusing to see him up on his toes, his arms curved, mingling the aesthetic of the dancing master with that of the painter, speaking of the "delicate dustman" of Velasquez and the "silhouettes" of Mantegna. A real character, this Degas, sickly, neurotic, an ophthalmic to the

68

68   Edgar Degas: *Dances in the Rehearsal Hall.* 1889-1893. Oil on canvas, 56.5 x 82.5 cm. New York, Private collection

69   Edgar Degas: *Dancers Backstage.* c. 1880. Distemper and pastel, 66.5 x 47 cm. New York, Private collection

No social message from Degas, to whom the dancer was a "tool." Whether he depicted dancers or laundresses, it was their movement that interested him. He loved movement that shifted line and color. "They call me the painter of dancers; they don't realize that for me dancers are a good excuse to paint beautiful fabrics and to show movement."

point where he fears for his sight [actually he will lose it]; but by the same token an eminently sensitive being who is feeling the repercussion of things. He is the one, of all whom I have seen up to now, who has best caught the soul of modern life in his depiction of it."

Like a photographer, Degas takes quick snapshots, focusing on his dancers, freezing them in a pose. Sometimes he brings his lens so close that he cuts them in half (ill. 69). The paradox of this technique is his abstraction. Degas's dancers "are not women at all," wrote Valéry, "but beings of a peerless substance, translucent and sensitive, their flesh of glass, madly provoking, canopies of floating silks." "I have always tried," Degas would say of the Impressionists, "to urge my colleagues to seek new combinations in the medium of drawing, which I consider more fruitful than that of color. But they wouldn't listen to me and have gone in other directions." To the mother of Ludovic Halévy he said, "Louise, I would have liked to make your portrait, you are so very drawable. . ." It was to break our habits of seeing that Degas undertook to catch the world of dancers from the most surprising angles. "A picture is something which necessitates as much trickery and vice as the perpetration of a crime; cheat, and add a spice of character." Often the dancers are shown in clusters with wide

70 Edgar Degas: *Dancers in Pink.*
c. 1895. Pastel, 68 x 56 cm. New York,
Private collection

71 Edgar Degas: *Dancer with a Red
Shawl.* c. 1889. Pastel, 64 x 49 cm.
U.S.A., Private collection

gaps of empty space encroaching on the picture (ill. 68). The ground can become
the most essential part of the composition. What Edmond de Goncourt called
"the little monkey girls" pursue "their graceful shuffling" around the edges of
the large untouched area cleared by the artist. He had recourse to the most
varied techniques, and after canvas he chose as a base lightly sized papers or
ones rubbed with oil, on these he painted with colors diluted with gasoline. He

liked pastel (ill. 69-71) to be "very lightly applied to slightly glazed paper. It's very vibrant. It's a good medium." Mixing it with other methods, he produced that alchemy which makes his dancers so weightless, so remote.

V   The artificial life

Degas, followed later by Toulouse-Lautrec, took his camera-brush or camera-pencil everywhere, and the "negatives" thus accumulated constituted, as did Balzac's stories, a *Human Comedy*.

"You must have real life, I want artificial life," said Degas to his friends. From 1869 onwards he did, indeed, prefer the artificial light of theatres, cafés, and music halls to the open air. He liked to catch the professional gestures of his subjects and to astound the viewer by his surprising angles and point of focus. He had done quite a lot of photography, and his practiced eye determined the layouts that would make many illustrated journals famous today and shower honors on their photographers. He has left us his definition of the ideal studio: "Place tiers all round the room so that you can draw things from above and below. Only paint things seen in a mirror, so that you get accustomed to disliking trompe-l'oeil. To do a portrait, have the sitter pose on the ground floor and paint on the floor above, so that you can train yourself to retain shapes and expressions; never draw or paint immediately."

A frequent visitor of his, Paul Valéry, said: "His art may be compared to that of the moralists; the cleanest prose shaping or forcefully articulating a new and accurate observation." There is, in fact, something of the moralist in Degas; his drawing is intended to accent, as much by his choice of subject as by his method of execution, the remorseless emphasis on the artificiality of the scenes he depicts: *The Absinthe Drinker* (ill. 74), brothel scenes in which he was ahead of Toulouse-Lautrec. But among his preoccupations with translating the life of society, he was especially interested, he notes in his catalogue, in the study of different kinds of smoke, and in reflections. He thought that those reflections of glass lamps in the mirrors of cafés would offer material for interesting variations and he would realize such ideas in his impressions of music halls or café concerts (ill. 72). Photographic proofs have been found for many of his pictures, which show that he made many shots until he was finally satisfied that he had the right setting and layout, and this he would later reproduce exactly in the painting. Degas was also one of the first collectors of Japanese prints— Hokusai, Hiroshige, Utamaro, and Hayashi. He found them particularly interesting for their off-focus composition and foreshortening, the cutting right to the edge, the techniques which emphasized large planes and helped to bring the eye of the viewer closer to the subject. Photography, like Japanese prints, enabled him to study tilted angles and the means to render the composition of the scene most effectively. Also, like a photographer, he played with spotlights, and did not do any favors to his subjects. Singers, actors, ballet dancers are all lit from below, and the faces coated with makeup, the long sparkling gowns and costumes appear in fantastic unreality against the darkness.

In the series *The Comedians*, Daumier had already rendered the distortion of faces and expressions under the footlights. We can see the same method at work in *The Chess Players* (ill. 76). Sometimes, with both these artists, the emphasis seems like an accusation.

In contrast to these two, Manet appears to be very kind to his subject in *The Waitress* (ill. 73). With this picture he continued his naturalistic series, begun with *Nana*, the courtesan, and continued with *The Plum*, which is a powerful depiction of the destructive effects of absinthe (cf. Degas, ill. 74). Beyond the

72 **Edgar Degas:** *Café Concert at Les Ambassadeurs.* **1876-1877. Pastel on monotype, 37 x 27 cm. Lyons, Musée des Beaux-Arts**

Degas was as obsessed by light as his friends were, but he preferred the artificial light of the theater, the circus, or the café, or lamplight falling on a bed or wallpaper.

story it tells, we are swept away by its brilliance. We should say, by the way, that it was not Zola who inspired Manet, but that on the contrary the canvas preceded the novel. About *Nana* Gustave Geffroy wrote: "Everything here speaks of the faubourgs and the boulevards, the indifference and the vice of Paris, and everything is rounded off by the presence of the man, the super-numerary of the 'great life.'" Similarly Huysmans speaks of Brussels in *The Artist*: ". . . needless to say that morning and night they crowd before this canvas, that it evokes indignant cries and the laughter of the mob made stupid by those blinds which Cabanel, Bouguereau, Toulmouche, and others think necessary to daub and display on the walls in the spring of each year."

For Cézanne, the gaming activities of *The Card Players* (ill. 75) were not devoid of significance either. The thesis advanced by Sabine Cotté seems plausible: at that time Cézanne was preoccupied with *The Bathers* which represented for him the pure idyllic imagery of a man freed from the dross of everyday life, in direct communication with nature. In a sort of antithesis, *The Card Players* represents the kind of confrontation to which man as a social being is subjected, even in the course of a simple game.

For Renoir, "the painter of happiness," life is never artificial. With *Dance in the City* (ill. 78) and *Dance in the Country* (ill. 77), as Jean-Louis Vaudoyer has noted, "It's not a question of two models passively posing, but rather of two human beings who live one memorable moment of their existence." It is what separates, among other things, academic art from that of the Impressionists. In *Dance in the Country*, he has posed his future wife, Aline Charigot, and his friend the painter, Paul Lhote. For *Dance in the City* he used a young acrobat, Maria Clementine, who later became known under the pseudonym of Suzanne Valadon. These two superb and inseparable works, owned for a long time by the Durand-Ruel family, have just been added to the Louvre collections.

Federico Fellini, who is in a similar business, and whose Giulietta might be a sister to Grille-d'Egout or Nini Patte-en-l'air, renders homage to Toulouse-Lautrec thus: "This aristocrat detested the beau monde, and he believed that the most beautiful and unsullied flowers grew in wastelands and public dumps." It is quite true that in his time Lautrec was not forgiven for what can still shock people today—his complete absence of prejudice, his complete ease with what are conventionally called vice or virtue. He is not a moralist like Degas, he is an accomplice. "If I weren't a painter," he said, "I would be a doctor or a surgeon." He is not a *voyeur*, like Degas, but simply an observer. Lautrec is never cruel, except momentarily. "Oh how badly you have treated me, you little monster," scrawled Yvette Guilbert at the bottom of a canvas which immortalized her and which she sent back to him. She reproached him for his caricature of her face, but he had seen only the black gloves in flight, those fluttering wings of which he had executed many rough sketches, with machine-gun swiftness.

For Toulouse-Lautrec, beauty was movement, life, the absence of moral or physical constraints. It was the same movement which attracted Degas, the transformation that accompanies motion. Both invented a technique for themselves, the one to enable him to retain on paper the magic of the image, the other to enable him to draw faster. Degas tried distemper or paste, egg or gouache, one after the other, to try to rediscover the matte finish of Italian frescoes. He even tried adding highlights of gold or silver to the gouache or watercolor in order to paint fans directly on the silk. He tried pastel, spraying it with boiling water, and thus obtaining a paste which he worked with his brush or a wash which he spread, according to the thickness or thinness. Lautrec invented his personal technique for going more quickly, diluting his colors with gasoline so that they would dry more rapidly. He chose tinted papers which would serve as already prepared grounds and have color value. No need now to waste time in the application of several coats of color. The chosen ground showed between the brushstrokes. In order to translate the magical effects of the light projectors on the veils of Loïe Fuller (ill. 79), which seemed to give them multicolored movement, he made a print which he touched up with watercolor and dusted with gold powder.

Watchful, perched on a bar stool or leaning on a marble-topped table, Lautrec awaited his prey: a woman, a dog, a glove, a stocking, a couple, a dress, a ribbon, everything or anything that might belong to a man or a woman.

75

76

74   Edgar Degas: *The Absinthe Drinker.* 1876. Oil on canvas, 92 x 68 cm. Paris, The Louvre

75   Paul Cézanne: *The Cardplayers.* c. 1885-1890. Oil on canvas, 47.3 x 56 cm. Paris, Musée d'Orsay , Galerie du Jeu de Paume

76   Honoré Daumier: *The Chess Players.* 1863. Oil on canvas, 248 x 320 cm. Paris, Musée du Petit Palais

False paradises and alcohol, the slow killer, are subjects dear to Manet and Degas. Man against man, even in play, is a theme which Cézanne did five times, using the peasants of Aix for his models. He may have been inspired by Le Nain's *The Cardplayers*, which is in the museum at Aix. Daumier treated the same subject with his characteristic mixture of power and simplicity.

77 Pierre-Auguste Renoir: *Dance in the Country.* 1883. Oil on canvas, 180 x 90 cm. Paris, Musée d'Orsay, Galerie du Jeu de Paume

78 Pierre-Auguste Renoir: *Dance in the City.* 1883. Oil on canvas, 180 x 90 cm. Paris, Musée d'Orsay, Galerie du Jeu de Paume

Renoir now outlined his forms firmly and gave them a glossy finish. He made many preparatory drawings the same size as the proposed picture and traced them carefully. He no longer concerned himself with evoking the subject by the use of color; it was the line that mattered. His backgrounds remained the same as before, built up with tiny touches of color, and the strongly outlined figures in the foreground stood out all the more. It is this period of pearly flesh and delicate materials that is most sought after by collectors.

79

79 Henri de Toulouse-Lautrec: *Loïe Fuller at the Folies Bergères*. 1893. Oil on canvas, 63 x 45 cm. Albi, Musée Toulouse-Lautrec

80 Henri de Toulouse-Lautrec: *At the Moulin Rouge*. 1892. Oil on canvas, 123 x 141 cm. The Art Institute of Chicago (Helen Birch Bartlett Memorial Collection)

On the watch, behind his brush-camera, Lautrec took aim. If Degas used spotlights, we might say that Lautrec used a flash. Seated with a glass of sweet warm wine before him, he watched the "mecs" and the "darones" and then drew them, putting himself also into the picture. But what he watched and drew most avidly and most often was a little sixteen-year old blonde—we see her here in the background, tidying her hair—named Louise, nicknamed La Goulue. Like the artist, she had a voracious appetite for life, which with her natural ease and bursting energy she epitomized.

It was the new discovery of electric light, and the multi-colored spotlights that made the filmy veils of LoIe Fuller come alive.

81 | 82

81　Eugene Boudin: *Lady in White on the Beach at Trouville.* 1869. Oil on board, 32 x 49 cm. Le Havre, Musée des Beaux-Arts André Malraux

82　Claude Monet: *Camille Monet and Her Cousin on the Beach at Trouville.* 1870. Oil on canvas, 30 x 46 cm. Paris, Musée Marmottan

Boudin and Jongkind each in turn fostered in the young Monet a taste for luminous transparency, the magic of atmospheric variation. Monet was seventeen when Boudin, the master of sand and sky, chose him as a companion. "At his request" said Monet, "I went to work in the open air with him: I bought a paint-box and we were off to Rouelles, though without much conviction on my part. Boudin set up his easel and began to work. I looked at him apprehensively, then more attentively, and suddenly it was as though a veil was torn from my eyes—I realized, I grasped what painting could be. By this one example, my destiny as a painter was clear."

These two beach scenes, painted at Trouville, show how the master and his pupil are worthy of each other.

VI   Water, reflection of a reflection

Monet said about water: "I would like to be always looking at it, or upon it, and when I die, I would like to be buried in a buoy."

"Sunday, 12 December 1854: as always the light is poor, always gloomy. I have made five attempts to capture that delicacy and charm of it which is everywhere. There is a coolness, it is gentle, faded, and slightly rosy. Objects seem drowned in it. The sea was wonderful; the sky was smooth and velvety, afterwards it became yellowish; it was hot and the declining sun cast beautiful violet shadows over everything." These lines are not by Monet, they are by Eugène Boudin, but the study of color nuances was already on the Impressionist agenda.

One of Boudin's works—actually an academic one—*Le Pardon de Sainte-Anne-la Palud* sent to the Salon of 1859, caught the attention of Baudelaire. Subsequently, the painter, the son of a seaman, born at Honfleur, showed him many hundreds of pastels, all with the time of day and the wind direction recorded, devoted exclusively to waves and clouds. Baudelaire prophesied that Boudin "will display, in his finished pictures, a wonderful enchantment of air and water." His infatuation with the fleeting changes of atmosphere, with the play of light upon water, with the dazzle of dresses in beach scenes (ill. 81), make him incontestably a precursor of the Impressionists. Monet would willingly acknowledge their debt to him. Boudin's seascapes were seen by the young Oscar (Monet's given names were Oscar Claude, and he signed his earliest works "Oscar") displayed in front of his caricatures in the window of the shop where both of their work was on show. Oscar was proud to be paid ten francs—even occasionally a whole napoleon—for his caricatures. Boudin approached the young prodigy with much kindness; and, coming to serious matters, said: "That's very good for a beginning, but you shouldn't delay raising your prices. Study, learn to see and to paint, draw, make landscapes." Here an important word was dropped, one around which the life of Claude Monet would revolve for three-quarters of a century, a magic word, suffused with triumph and with suffering, with defeat and with immortality. His first impulse, if we are to believe Monet himself, was resentment; he didn't care for that man; he felt him to be sincere, but all he offered was endless labor, while Monet's short career as a caricaturist had brought him intoxication with his own talents and gold pieces in his woollen stocking. However, he yielded, he listened to his instincts, he followed the suggestion of that generous teacher who shared his discoveries with him; the lesson bore fruit: "My eyes are opened at last," he would say, "and I really understand nature; I have also learnt to love her."

Jongkind, another painter of seascapes, was also to influence Claude Monet and contribute to a learning common to Monet and the Impressionists, "to look on water as a lover." (Zola) A Dutchman who had come to live in France, Jongkind explored and painted along the Channel coast. He brought back drawings, watercolors (ill. 86), canvases that make him an immediate precursor of the Impressionists. He excels at evoking, as they were to do, the play of light, the extension of space, the instability of water. His landscapes are allied with those of Corot and Daubigny, but his seascapes already show the pale sea green harmonies which directly catch the clarity of hour and place. Jongkind, extolled by the Impressionists without ever participating in their exhibitions, pushed the fragmenting of his strokes and the freedom of his composition a long way, easily suggesting the unfinished. Daniel Wildenstein, who had a detailed knowledge of Monet's life, tells us of the historic meeting between the two.

83   **H. de Bréval:** *On the Beach.* **1879. Oil on canvas, 43.5 x 60 cm. Paris, Private collection**

While the Impressionists chose to snatch the ephemeral, to capture a fleeting atmosphere, the Academicians were content merely to relate an anecdote.

83

Monet, who had just been relieved of military service—his family had offered a substitute for him—swore only by painting and the sunlit sea, his faithful mistress! He was in the middle of a pastel, but his model, a cow, wouldn't stay still. A tall, lanky Englishman offered to hold it, and while struggling with the cow asked if he were acquainted with Jongkind. "Oh, yes," said Monet: "he's a painter of great talent." Well, if you would like to see him," continued the Englishman, "come here tomorrow and work in the field." "I was skeptical," Monet recounted, "but intrigued all the same; I came back. Jongkind arrived accompanied by the Englishman. Almost immediately he began to address me familiarly and we were already friends." Monet invited Jongkind to his home.

84

84 Pierre-Auguste Renoir: *La Gre-nouillère*. c. 1869. Oil on canvas, 66 x 81 cm. Stockholm, Nationalmuseum

The gallant fellow presented himse' together with Madame Fesser, that excellent woman whom he had rescued from starvation. When they were seated at the table the unsophisticated Dutchman thought he should say that his companion was not his wife. This to that virtuous head of family, Monet! They then began a series of excursions to the beach. Monet was particularly impressed by the direct and vigorous manner in which his new friend tackled that subject. "From that moment on, he was my true teacher," he would say. "It's to him that I owe the ultimate education of my eyes."

"Water is the earth's gaze, its means of looking at the weather," wrote Claudel. Degas thought, "One must keep on looking at everything, the big boats and the little boats, the movement of people both on the water and ashore. It's the movement of people and things which entertains and even consoles us. If the leaves on the trees didn't move, how sad the trees would be, and so would we!" This fondness for movement, where could it be better satisfied than on the water? In this area, Monet's stature is higher than all the others, but he was not the only one attracted by water. "There are a great many of us here at the moment, at Honfleurs," he wrote on 26 August 1864. Besides many "very bad painters, a lot of fools, we have a pleasant little circle. Jongkind and Boudin are here, we get along wonderfully and we never stop." Two of Monet's seascapes were accepted by the jury of the Salon of 1863: *The Mouth of the Seine at Honfleur* and *Hève Point at Low Tide*, seascapes which brought a substantial breath of fresh air into all the babbling allegories and bituminous models of the academicians. It was a real success, and Paul Mantz, in the *Gazette des Beaux-*

85 Claude Monet: *La Grenouillère.* 1869. Oil on canvas, 74.6 x 99.7 cm. New York, The Metropolitan Museum of Art

Together Renoir and Monet painted the same view of the water, on the same day at the same time, each according to his own disposition. In Monet's work less attention is paid to the figures and more given to the water. Renoir, on the other hand, concentrated on the details of the scene. The former has more power, the latter more delicacy.

Arts, presented to his readers "a new name, that of M. Claude Monet." Visitors who were either being facetious or were simply ill-informed congratulated Manet on a canvas from the brush of Monet: "Your picture's wonderful, old boy," and Manet complained, "Oh, my dear friend, it's disgusting. I am furious. They are congratulating me on a picture which isn't mine. It must be a hoax." "But in God's name, there are only about four of us who are capable of doing such a piece!" It was by something in this strain, if Zola is to be believed, that Daubigny, a member of the jury, welcomed Monet's *Ship Leaving the Pier at Le Havre* to the Salon of 1868.

This aquatic progress brings us to the culminating point of Impressionism, the simultaneous painting by Monet and by Renoir of *La Grenouillère* (ill. 84, 85). It could be said that at that time the two friends were not only on water but also on dry bread. Their material situation was hardly brilliant and according to

86 Johann-Barthold Jongkind: *The Lighthouse at Honfleur.* **1864. Watercolor, 22.9 x 46.3 cm. Paris, Private collection**

86 Johann-Barthold Jongkind: *The Lighthouse at Honfleur.* **1864. Watercolor, 22.9 x 46.3 cm. Paris, Private collection**

Jongkind's watercolors express an almost melancholy feeling of the light (B. Dorival). He knew how to convey the impalpable transparency of the air by his light, nervous strokes. Picking up from where Boudin left off, Monet recalled, "he made me show him my sketches and invited me to work with him, explaining how and why he did what he did, and completing Boudin's teaching, he was henceforward my real master."

86

87

87 Ernest Meissonier: *The Banks of the Seine at Poissy.* **1889. Oil on canvas, 15 x 23.8 cm. Paris, The Louvre**

Breaking away from the long series of musketeers and noblemen, Meissonnier, whom Degas called "the giant of the dwarfs," tried out the Impressionists' themes. Baudelaire, however, was not deceived and called him a Fleming without imagination, charm, a sense of color, or simplicity.

Renoir: "I am almost always at Monet's and, by the way, we are getting old. We don't get a bite to eat everyday. But I'm really quite happy because Monet is such a good painting companion." We know the result of this painting in partnership, the two famous *Grenouillères*, which the two masters executed elbow to elbow. This marked an important stage in the evolution of their art, at the same time as it bore witness to that extraordinary world of boating-parties and girls which Maupassant would celebrate in his stories. Of the two friends, Monet was the more creative, according to the evidence. He had arrived at the threshold of Impressionism, having learned the greater part of his new tricks of technique. The water was what mattered most to Monet. "With him," noted Zola, "water is a living thing, profound, and above all, genuine. It laps around the boats." His people are extremely simplified, almost abstract. Renoir, on the

contrary, tends to lose himself in detail. The brushstrokes of Monet are firmer, cleaner, and the contrast of color and tone is more accentuated. Renoir's representation is more delicate, less energetic, less well composed. Monet's canvas is witness to his complete mastery.

What Monet would see all his life through water, was the world as a reflection, the image of an image, the mirror and sheen of a magic prism that led, inexorably, to the liquid grays of the *Water Lilies* at the end. An inside-out world, unstable, distorted or effaced by any movement of the water. And, as noted by Jean Clay, he dared to treat the fluid as the solid, and movement by thick rectangular strokes.

Ever since the myth of Orpheus, artists have tried to enter the mirror. What better means than water to give the world an image of itself? Reflections are a constant and fundamental theme of Impressionism. Through reflections, the

89 Claude Monet: *Impression, Sunrise.*
1873. Oil on canvas, 48 x 63 cm. Paris,
Musée Marmottan

90 Joseph Mallord William Turner:
Keelman Heaving in Coals by Night.
1835. Oil on canvas, 90.2 x 121.9 cm.
Washington, National Gallery of Art
(Widener Collection)

Legend has it that Turner died shortly
before Christmas, standing at his window and watching the sun sink in the
mist. He has been called the Father of
the Impressionists and then the Father
of the Abstract Painters, which is
another way of saying that he defies la-
belling. We tend to overlook the under-
lying structure of his work, in which he
most closely resembles Cézanne. As for
Monet's picture, *Impression,* which gave
the movement its name, although
painted at Le Havre, it looks very much
like the Thames.

painter can take all kinds of liberties with nature, all with the air of simultaneously submitting himself to it. Reflections free artists from the necessity of contour and can break up the most static mass. Finally, reflections can permit the most unexpected combinations of color: in the foreground of *La Grenouillère*, the browns, blues, blacks, and yellows, are juxtaposed with a freedom and ease almost unknown in European art up to that time.

But what impudence, to dare to paint a popular scene of water and boats when the museums are full of the exploits of the gods, thanks to the efforts of conventional artists! It was this kind of picture, however, which enabled the Impressionists to make landscape the most important genre.

La Grenouillère was a restaurant and bathing place, situated on a small branch of the Seine, between Chatou and Bougival. It was chiefly frequented by artists, students, boating parties, and pretty girls, who met for dancing and bathing on Sundays and holidays. Maupassant often took this environment as a setting for his stories. "It was like a perpetual fiesta, and what a mixture of people there was!" Renoir would later tell his dealer, Ambroise Vollard. "People still knew how to laugh then. The machine hadn't taken over our lives, we had time to live and we didn't spare it." For the common people, care, misery, and grief stopped at the door of the ballroom and the water's edge. People drank white wine and ate fried food, they boated and lost their hats in the undergrowth near the landing places. According to Renoir, La Grenouillère was so named not because the place in fact resembled a swamp, but because in the slang of the period, "Grenouilles" (little frogs) was the term used to designate the young women, the little working girls, who came to pass the summer Sundays there with their stalwart companions.

"It was at La Grenouillère," Kenneth Clark was to say, "that Impressionism was truly born." A turn of the wheel, and Manet, who had so influenced the

91 Paul Gauguin: *Rocks in the Sea.* 1886. Oil on canvas, 73 x 92 cm. Private collection

91

92 Georges Seurat: *Le Bec du Hoc. Grandcamp*, 1885. Oil on canvas, 64.5 x 81.3 cm. London, Tate Gallery

Sea, sky and rocks were an ideal testing ground for someone like Gauguin, who had not yet found his style, as well as for a Seurat who made his of mathematical equations.

Impressionists, was in his turn influenced by them. He had already painted seascapes, ports, beaches, borrowing, for example, from Jongkind for his *Moonlight on the Port of Boulogne*, a study of night almost entirely in one color. With an economy of means and a scorn for easy effects, Manet had created an atmosphere that the works of the Impressionists would attempt to render yet more palpable. Henceforth Manet would study his pupil Monet, in order to learn the virtues of the color of light. It also represented a shift in the moral evolution of the painter. Before 1870 he was painting his friends and intimates in the studio. Thereafter he abandoned the museum and Salon subjects and distinguished models for everyday subjects and the leisure activities of the people and the demimonde. Under the influence of the naturalistic novel, Manet's brush began to keep low company, as formerly banished literature made a vigorous return. More than ever, Manet wanted to be the "painter of modern life." More than ever he was angrily booed by a public on whom his new style produced the effect of a red rag on a bull. As Monet and Pissarro had done after their sojourn in England, he went to Holland and had a similar revelation before Franz Hals as he had had before Velasquez in Vienna in 1856. Even more than the Impressionists had done, Franz Hals made him a convert to rapidity of execution. The so-called "black" period was left behind for the open air and a Debussy-like striking of chords; he had a certain spiritual relationship with the composer. The painting of his junior, *Camille Monet and her Cousin on the Beach at Trouville* (ill. 82), which sings like a fragment of music, echoes *On the Beach*, which summarizes Manet's new talent for recording eternal moments and translating the idea which haunted him, the concept of light. The composition also reflects Japonism, which had a continuing effect on his work.

Following the direction of Monet, Manet painted moving water. Monet, now in the grip of his passion, painted from his boat-studio, an old boat which he had bought at the instigation of Daubigny, and which allowed him to set up his easel anywhere in his favorite element. He installed himself at Argenteuil, where the upper crust of Impressionism came to join him; besides Manet, there were Sisley and Renoir. Argenteuil at that time presented an unparalleled setting, with its widened riverbed and a dock which offered the boating parties an ideal field for their exercises; upstream two bridges spanned the Seine. One, quite straight, carried the railroad; the other which bore the road, saw mirrored in the water its elegant arches. A painter of water above all else, Monet was

93

fascinated by the Seine; its barges, its bridges, its promenade, its sailing boats, its canal boats, all are found in his canvases, and are shown from a great variety of angles, thanks to the boat-studio that gave him such great freedom of movement. When the yachtsmen organized their regattas, the painter was there and caught on his canvas for eternity the big white sails unfolding against a clear sky. Cloudy weather did not discourage him, and it was with a sure hand that he set down on a turbulent Seine the sails bending before the breeze towards the red roofs of Petit-Gennevilliers.

Sisley was also a painter of water. But he was not only drawn to summer landscapes. He often turned to the depiction of floods. Already in 1872 he had studied the effects of the watery invasion of the island of the Loge and the St. Germain road at Port-Marly. In 1876 he painted the floods at Port-Marly. To do so he had only to walk down to the banks of the Seine, not far from his lodgings at no. 4 on the Abreuvoir road.

Whereas Monet, in his *Debacles,* had painted vast stretches covered with water and ice, seeking to give the effect of great desolation, which displayed his latent romanticism, Sisley thought the effects more dramatic in an inhabited area. In his *Flood at Port-Marly* (ill. 88) despite the tragic subject and the threatening skies, there is a kind of serene peace over the picture. This is because Sisley knew how to imbue things with his humanity. The possibility that the waters might well rise ominously and inundate everything did not prevent the painter from noting the exquisite harmony of the creams and ochres of the Nicolas house, and the gradations of blues and greens of sky and water, nor from foretelling the arrival of spring in the young shoots on the bare trees. With his wonderfully sensitive eye, Sisley perceived the most delicate harmonies of nature and succeeded in catching them on canvas.

Monet's influence on the group is indisputable. When Paul Alexis proposed to organize a "trade union of artists," it was Monet who responded in the name of this "group of Naturalists, with the legitimate ambition to paint nature and life in a broad reality." The negotiations ended in the creation of a "private artists' cooperative" and the organization, far removed from the official Salons, of a collective exhibition which opened its doors on 15 April 1874, on the premises of the photographer Nadar, at 35 Boulevard des Capuchins near the rue Danau. One hundred and sixty-five pictures were hung, but it was one of Monet's canvases which acted as both a symbol and as a target. It was through him that all the fuss came about.

This canvas, a seascape painted at Le Havre, Monet had entitled, *Impression, Sunrise* (ill. 89). A critic picked this up, and surpassing his colleagues in spiteful irony, called his article "Exhibition of the Impressionists." The name stuck. In *The Charivari* one could read, "*Impression*, of that I am sure. I also told myself that since I was impressed, there must have been an impression somewhere in there . . . And so much freedom and ease in the composition! Marbled paper in its most embryonic state is more finished than that seascape!" Castagnary understood better: "They are Impressionists in the sense that they do not depict the landscape, but rather the feeling produced by the landscape." Nevertheless, if this picture gave its name to Impressionism, we should recognize that it is first of all a recollection of what Monet had seen in the London museums. It is less of an impression produced by nature than of a variation on a theme dear to Whistler or Turner (ill. 90). In Le Havre one can recognize the Thames. It foretells the famous views of London which were to come.

"You are the Raphael of water," Manet said to him. Monet observed how water behaved at wave-top level. He liked it to become hazy—as in *Impression*—he also liked it to become smoky and mingle with that of the railroad. Metaphorical water fascinated him; leaves and grass became little waves. Later on, he would work at transforming the cathedral at Rouen or the Doge's Palace into water. One never knows with him where water begins and ends. As a painter he is interested in mixing the elements, in depicting the reflections of vegetation in the river, and he succeeded in achieving a harmony of blues and greens, each looking like the other, thanks to his famous technique. The tremor of the waves is imparted to the sky, which itself becomes a liquid element. The whole picture, like *Boats, Regatta at Argenteuil* becomes a fluid wall, which will also be the case with the *Water Lilies.* The littleness of man, and the immutable

94 Gustave Courbet: *The Waves.* 1869.
Oil on canvas, 73 x 150 cm. Philadelphia Museum of Art

95 Gustave Courbet: *Marine Landscape.* 1874. Oil on canvas, 46 x 55 cm.
USA, Private collection

96 Claude Monet: *Waterlily Pond and
Bridge.* 1905. Oil on canvas, 95 x 100
cm. Private collection

Even Courbet, the Realist, became almost an abstractionist when confronted
by the sea. One has to step back a little,
as with Monet's pictures, before one can
really distinguish the sea and the sky.
Courbet himself once had to do the same
before he could tell the subject of his
canvas—it was a bundle of sticks! Always generous, Courbet consistently
helped his juniors. Monet recalled that
he was ever helpful and encouraging,
even to the point of lending money in
difficult times.

97

97 Claude Monet: *Waterlilies, Study of Water at Sunset.* Painted at Giverny, 1914-1918. Oil on canvas, 197 x 594 cm. Paris, The Louvre

98 Jackson Pollock: *Painting.* 1948. Oil on canvas, 61 x 80 cm. Paris, Musée national d'art moderne, Pompidou Center

greatness of nature. What better illustration of this than a rock, thrust up like a mountain through the waves? A coalescence of being with primeval chaos. The varied cliffs of Etretat, with their immense flying buttresses, lend themselves to thoughts of this kind. Delacroix, Corot, Courbet, and Monet devoted themselves to them. Those rocks seem to rear up until even the pictures seems too small for them.

Before becoming the "real" Gauguin, the Tahitian one, that painter would have to shake the earth off his sabots. Brittany gave him a solid basis for his final flowering (ill. 91). He was conscious there of a direct communion with nature: "I love Brittany: there I find the wild and the primitive. When my boots

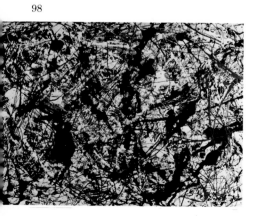

echo on that granite surface, I hear a heavy, dull, powerful sound, and that's what I look for in painting." The question now to be faced was how to escape Impressionism. A meeting with the young Emile Bernard was decisive. He also wished to avoid Impressionism and sought to reconcile his art with the ideas of the fledgling symbolist poetry. Bernard's search for a synthesis of the simplification of color and form was in direct opposition to Impressionism, which was a means of analysis. His ambition to give to a picture a spiritual significance going beyond the simple evocation of nature was too similar to Gauguin's concerns for the two men not to feel an immediate interest in each other. It seems likely that it was Emile Bernard who first had the idea of surrounding the forms in a drawing with a thick line to separate the colors from each other and to give an accentuated rhythm to the composition.

Another way to avoid Impressionism was to codify it by making systematic laws. That is what Seurat tried to do. At the same time as he elaborated his drawing technique, he also, especially from the beginning of 1882, executed what he called his "rough oil sketches." These were notations in oil on a small panel or piece of canvas, which he fixed to the underside of the lid of his color box and which measured 16 by 26 cm. There, trying out his color formulas, he transformed these small sketches into finished works. As were the Impressionists, he was attracted by the reflections of water, by the shady banks of the Seine, by the glimmer of the river through the branches, by the bulky mass of a barge, and the tapered lightness of the canoes. He seemed like a one-man anthology of all art: like the Romantics, he tinted the horizon with red at sunset; like Corot, he seemed to dissolve light foliage into the air. He reminded one of Manet

It is tempting to make a bridge—a Japanese one, preferably—between the "large decorations" of Monet and the huge "drippings" of Pollock. Such a relationship was established *a posteriori* by the Americans, always seeking their origins, by making Pollock the spiritual son of Monet, and Impressionism the father of Abstract Expressionism. In letting the paint run directly onto the canvas from a pierced container, Pollock, sometimes drunk, wanted to get inside

when he painted a garden, of Jongkind when he depicted a riverbank, of Monet when he arranged the ears of corn in a wheatfield. He was more absorbed in experimenting with values than with colors. In *Le Bec du Hoc* (ill. 92), Seurat was already practicing the separation of colors into their elements. He endeavored to give the effect of light with his clear colors. His shadows are less strong in his paintings than in his drawings, but in *Bec du Hoc* they nevertheless allow the sea to extend to the horizon. "This transformation of Impressionism," wrote Paulet, "is interesting to take cognizance of: it marks the beginning of abandonment to pure sensation. The line, that's the purpose. In spite of themselves, painters keep returning to it, it is such a fertile source." Seurat carried out the precept that "painting is the art of excavating a surface." The wish to give a meaning to line was not anything new: it had been established in the sixteenth and seventeenth centuries. Seurat also came under the influence of Japanese prints, appreciating their purity of outline and color. According to

the canvas. In the chaos which resulted, perhaps Pollock was trying to catch a changing reflection of our world.

certain writers, he also went so far as to plagiarize the Japanese masters: the *Bec du Hoc* could be a rerendering of Hokusai's *The Wave*. Humbert de Superville's *Essay on the Unqualified Signs of Art* was well known to Seurat. That writer regarded the horizontal as expressing calm, rising lines showed energy or joy, descending lines, sadness or loss. It was what Henry called dynamogeny. Fénéon could write in 1889, "M. Seurat knows very well that a line, independently of its topographical role, possesses an appraisable abstract value. In each of his landscapes the shapes are governed by one or two directions; linked by dominant tints with which the subordinate lines are obliged to contrast."

99

It is certain that Seurat's pointilliste method was far from universally accepted. Even Pissarro, who rallied to the Neo-Impressionists, expressed doubts: "What to do to obtain the qualities of purity, of the utmost simplicity, the suppleness, the freedom, the spontaneity, the freshness of feeling of our Impressionist art? That's the question I am very much preoccupied with, because the thing is so unsubstantial, inconsistent, airy, unvarying rather than simple, especially the Seurats, the Seurats above all." Seurat himself was well aware of the problem. At Port-en-Bassin he painted with wide brushstrokes which remained visible under the dotted spaces with which he covered them. He stylized rather than fragmented. Renoir, Monet, and Sisley would withdraw from the eighth and last Impressionist exhibition as a protest when they learned that Seurat would show there.

Thus, the more fame it achieved, the more Impressionism tended towards abstraction. The basic theme of *Marseilles, seen from l'Estaque* was the object of Cézanne's research in the years 1882-1887. He did not intend to make a realistic translation of the landscape; on the contrary, he intended an abstraction. He availed himself of the masses of the water and mountains to give a feeling of space and volume. For him, the sea had the solidity of enamel. Unlike Monet, he did not try to catch the variations of nature, but to show it as immutable. The Côte and its trees, its vegetation, its rocks, were for him all of the same nature as the sea, set in a balance of opposing forces. This titanic battle is expressed by the opposing masses and colors. "Nature is deeper when it comes to the surface," he said. In *The Lake at Annecy* (ill. 93), the water does not break up the reflections, as it does, for example, with Monet. Those rigid perpendicular lines, those solid vertical strokes which make up the reflections contradict the horizontality of the water. One is looking at a building game, but one devised, it would seem, by a gigantic superterrestrial hand. It is the principle of alienation and harmony. It is up to the viewer to do the work and discover the depth in these colors, these spots, these strokes which collide to make a universe. All Cubism will have to do is to send in the relieving troops. One can see in Impressionism Abstraction and Cubism waiting to emerge.

Courbet, already "the Raphael of the quarries" as Monet was of water, took real liberties with reality. In his seascapes also (ill. 94, 95), the sea was mingled with the sky, invading the whole canvas to make an almost abstract work. At the time, it was objected that "composition wasn't his strong point." However, André Fermigier explained the real truth: "To compose is already to transpose, to comment, to play with the truth for a moment, with the naked fact of 'positive, immediate nature,' with a reality whose whole force is related to its own insignificance. Courbet resists thinking or composing." The smallness of the little boats expresses the insignificance of the human presence in relation to the calm power of the elements.

Monet led the Impressionist enterprise to its end, and its end is actually abstraction. At the beginning of 1904, the landscape disappeared bit by bit, water occupied the whole surface of the canvas and suggested illimitable space.

"These landscapes of water and reflections have become an obsession," wrote Monet. The *Water Lilies* series (ill. 96, 97, 99), contemporaries of the beginnings of abstract art that Monet may well have been aware of, are actually, if one may believe the artist, a new manifestation of his attachment to realism, although their nonrealism is everywhere recognized.

Michel Hoog notes that "in order to paint these unrealistic canvases, Monet, traumatized by the reproaches he had encountered in his youth for the illegibility of his canvases, made himself an alibi by making a real garden at Giverny which resembled the one he wanted to paint." "My finest masterpiece is my garden," he said one day. It was nature remodeled by the artist that governed the inspiration of his last years. "More a true transposition of art than a model for a picture," (Marcel Proust). This garden at Giverny, maintained today in its former state, was created by Monet with his gardeners, changing the course of the stream, planting exotic flowers, and seeding the pond with water lilies. The Japanese bridge recalls Monet's admiration for Hokusai and Hiroshige. With a poet's intuition Claudel wrote in 1927, "Thanks to the water, he became the indirect painter of that which one cannot see." Quite a good definition of abstract art!

Untiringly Monet mingled the reflection of the sky, the transparent depths of the water, and the surface on which the lilies floated. The picture's magic is born from the mixture of those three spaces. The nineteen panels, each about four by two metres, placed in the rooms of the Orangerie, make the viewer feel he is wandering in a world without landmarks or signposts. He feels like a fish in an aquarium. "These canvases compel a fervent, single-minded attention bordering on the hypnotic," wrote Claude Roger-Marx. And Louis Gillet spoke of "this new way of identifying oneself with the universal elements."

In inventing the "dripping" technique, which consists of allowing colors from a pierced box to run directly onto the canvas, Jackson Pollock followed the logical development of the *Water Lilies* (ill. 98): "My painting," said the American artist, "doesn't come via the easel . . . I prefer to fasten the canvas to the flat wall or lay it out on the floor . . . then I feel closer to the painting, somehow a part of it. I can walk around it, work from all four sides, and literally get inside it." With Pollock, not only has the old image of man disappeared, but not a trace of him remains. All that is left are his strong vibrations.

VII   Weather landscapes

100   Alfred Sisley: *Snow at Louvençiennes.* 1878. Oil on canvas, 61 x 50.5 cm. Paris, The Louvre

101   Jean-Auguste-Dominique Ingres: *Raphael's House in Rome.* 1806. Oil on canvas, circular, 15 cm. diameter. Paris, Musée des Arts decoratifs

102   Camille Corot: *Rome, the Forum, View from the Farnese Gardens.* 1826. Paste paper on canvas, 28.8 x 50.4 cm. Paris, The Louvre

"I was painting some haystacks, which had caught my attention and which made a fine cluster, just a couple of steps away from here; one day, I saw that my light had changed. I said to my daughter-in-law: "Quick, run to the house and bring me another canvas, please." She brought me one, but in no time the light was all different again; another! and then another! I only worked at one of them as long as the impression was there. You can see what I mean."

Giverny, 1890, and Monet's long search for subjects had ended at that epoch. The procession of "series," haphazard until the *Rouen Cathedral* series (ill. 53, 54), became more and more systematic.

The Impressionists had captured the beauty of the seasons; now they were going on to catch the charm of the fleeting moment.

Ingres had already executed in Rome, at the Villa Borghese, three tiny circular landscapes whose luminosity presaged Corot, three views at three different times of day. *Raphael's House*, for example (1806, ill. 101), seems overwhelmed with the heat of the noonday sun. Ingres, who usually only used landscape as a background, as a symbol which defined the individuals he placed against it, managed, thanks to a stay in Italy, to paint deserted landscapes and catch their feeling exactly. For once, the human figure disappears, leaving only the landscape and its atmosphere.

It was also in Italy, so propitious for changes of weather, that Corot (before Monet and the Impressionists) had painted the same views from different aspects and at different times of day, in order to observe the effect of changing light upon shape and form. Thus, *Rome, the Forum, View from the Farnese Gardens* (1826; ill. 102) was painted at noon. Well before Cézanne, the amiable Corot, an unconscious revolutionary, went so far as to simplify the subject, to make the houses and monuments more geometrical in contrasting planes of light and dark. The gamut of tones used is sustained by the irridescence of the atmosphere and the modulation of the values. "This infallible feeling in Corot, so rare, seems less like a talent for seeing and more like a reflection of his soul," noted Jean Leymarie. He took up the compact, grainy craftsmanship of the Le Nain brothers, of Chardin, cementing the masses and harmonizing the values, and—like Vermeer, but with less magic and more flavor—impalpably distilling the subject matter and the light. In his *Rome: the Island and Bridge of San Bartolomeo*, of the same period, Corot is not content merely to carve out the strange cubist buildings of the island, hewn in facets like a diamond, but is also interested in creating the atmosphere with which they are suffused, the space in which they assume shape, a synthesis which will be the eternal quest of Cézanne.

Each Impressionist has his speciality. For Sisley, that creator of roads lost in infinity, it is the winter, because he was attracted by the intangible aspect of the snow. We know the difficulties the Impressionists had with depicting snow until the meeting with Turner. In the neighborhood of Sèvres, Sisley found the kind of snow he wanted. In all weathers he set up his easel at Suresnes, at Meudon, at Saint-Cloud and at Louvenciennes. In contrast to Renoir, who liked only green countryside and sunny beaches, and who called snow "that leper of nature," Sisley had a predilection for winter landscapes, in which some bare trees stand out on the white ground, and the gray sky speaks of sadness and the desolation of a benumbed countryside. One cannot admire too much the economy of means with which Sisley knew how to depict all the different whites of the snow, and how exactly he differentiated and emphasized the blue and

101

Ingres augured the sureness and luminosity of Corot when he painted his *Raphael's House,* where he paid particular attention to space and atmosphere—we should remember that he was above all a figure-painter. Baudelaire's definition of Realism, "the world without Man" can be applied to these unusual landscapes, painted simply for themselves and with all trace of people removed.

102

Like Monet after him, Corot painted the same scene from different angles and at different times. Long before Cézanne, in 1826, he simplified the subject and emphasized the geometrical shapes of the monuments and houses in contrasting shapes of light and shadow. In this respect, Jean Leymarie has alluded to Le Nain and Chardin as showing how Corot "built up the masses and harmonized their values" and to Vermeer for subject matter and light. It would be necessary to follow the course of the whole history of art in order to take account of the many channels which helped to irrigate the soil from which Impressionism sprung.

103

104

103 Harpignies: *Wooded Landscape at Sunset.* c. 1860-1865. Oil on canvas, 32 x 60 cm. England, Private collection

104 Alfred Sisley: *Fog at Voisins.* 1874. Oil on canvas, 50.5 x 65 cm. Paris, The Louvre

salmon pink shadows. In *Snow at Louvenciennes* (ill. 100), a woman is walking away from us down a road with walls on either side, and the artist has needed to do nothing more to suggest the extraordinary silence which encloses people and things when winter reigns.

Harpignies (ill. 103) was still under the influence of Corot when he left for Italy to try to capture the atmospheric feeling peculiar to that master. Théodore Rousseau (ill. 105), another painter of the Barbizon school, was well acquainted—perhaps too well—with the work of the English Romantics, particularly Bonington, and of the Dutch masters, and his originality would always be

105

106

105 Théodore Rousseau: *Wooded Landscape.* c. 1860. Oil on wood, 30 x 50 cm. Private collection

106 Camille Pissarro: *Kitchen Garden with Trees in Flower, Spring.* Pontoise, 1877. Oil on canvas, 65.5 x 81 cm. Paris, The Louvre

The Barbizon School (Diaz, Dupré, Millet, Rousseau, Harpignies, Daubigny) made a link with the Dutch tradition of the seventeenth century (Ruysdael, Hobbema, van Goyen, Groos, Van der Neer)

It was Boudin, Jongkind and Corot who taught Sisley to dilute the "tobacco-juice" colors of the Barbizon palette. Nevertheless, Barbizon had within it the seeds of the Impressionist revolution. Water, reflection, the insubstantial, so dear to Monet, were anticipated by Daubigny whose canal boat would later give Monet the idea for his floating studio. And it was Daubigny who introduced Monet to Paul Durand-Ruel in London in 1870, saying "Here's a young man who will be better than all of us."

limited by that fact. The least that remains from his journey round France, punctuated by canvases which bring together his favorite subjects—the sky, the play of light on water, trees—is that he showed the Impressionists which road to follow, where nature becomes the subject of painting.

Corot did not stint on advice to the young Pissarro. The affable old master, who kept no school, helped and guided him as he had done many others. Baudelaire described this teaching as "firm, bright, and methodical." It is undoubtedly true that the open and direct nature of Pissarro—he was always known for his frankness and integrity—gave much pleasure to the elder man.

But Pissarro is not Corot. He begins where his master left off (ill. 106). Cézanne maintained that all the Impressionists were indebted to Pissarro: "Already by 1865 he had eliminated the black, the bitumen, the Siena brown and the ochres. . . . Never, he said, use any colors except the primary ones and their direct derivatives." It was Cézanne who would render the greatest homage to him. At the peak of his glory, the master of Aix would choose, in an exhibition, to present himself as "Pissarro's pupil."

"Between our eye and the appearance of figures, seas, flowers, fields, the atmosphere is actually interposed," wrote Octave Mirbeau in the preface to an exhibition of Monet at the gallery of Georges Petit in 1889. "Each object is visibly suffused by the air, with its mysterious glaze which is the envelope for all the colors, sparkling or subdued, which it has gathered up before reaching us." Seeing the same subject at all hours of the day, and catching it in its infinite variety, led Monet to the idea of the series. Sometimes the effect was tossed off in a few moments. Seven minutes for one of the *Poplars* (ill. 107), Lilia Cabot-Perry reported. She saw a canvas to which the master had devoted only one sitting; it was covered with strokes six or seven millimeters long, separated by empty spaces of more than two centimeters. On a canvas that had had two sittings, the strokes were more numerous and closer together; the subject began to emerge more clearly. With the progress of the series, born by chance, raised to the rank of a system, the effort and the struggle did not disappear: only the excursions across the countryside ceased. Scientifically, Monet wanted his painting to register the modifications of reality occasioned by the color variations of the atmosphere. He wanted to make a synthesis of the atmosphere, but it couldn't be done. "I am in the middle of nature without being able to grasp it." *The Hayricks* (ill. 108-110) offered him the subject of the first series.

The Hayricks were exhibited at Durand-Ruel in May 1891, the *Poplars* series in March 1892. "It's a study of the same landscape, in mild weather, at different times of the day," wrote Gustave Geffroy. The series seemed to present themselves, one after the other. To Marcel Pays, who interviewed him for *Excelsior* in 1920, Monet confided: "You're not an artist if you don't have the picture in your head before you execute it, and if you aren't sure of your craft and composition . . . Techniques vary . . . Art stays the same: it's a transposition which is at the same time deliberate and yet responsive to nature." Paul Valéry would translate it thus: "Man lives and dies by what he sees, but he only sees what he dreams." Monet carried his pictures so firmly in his mind that he could not allow the models to be destroyed. When the poplars which he was painting were to be cut down by the parish of Limetz and sold, Monet went so far as to pay, in order to obtain a respite for them for some further time. This anecdote emphasizes the fascination which an unusual subject—and an inspirational one—had for him.

Monet was not content just to record the weather. To his work as a meteorologist he added that of a daring designer. Beyond the naturalist or pantheist interpretation which prevailed in Monet's circles, a modern glance would also find there the research for the layout of *The Hayricks*, the tendency towards geometrical abstraction of *The Poplars*. The proportions vary from one canvas to another. As essential to the work as the variables are the atmospheric observations that the artist gives to the course of the hours and days. Looking at *The Poplars*, Jean Clair dreamed of Mondrian. In front of *The Hayricks*, Kandinsky had a revelation. In 1895, on being shown one of the series, he received a jolt which would change the direction of his life.

While painting was on the way to abstraction—"A picture is an original combination of lines and tones that asserts itself," Degas was never tired of repeating—success overtook Monet. A quite considerable success, and the dithyrambic prose in which the critics greeted the *Poplars* and spoke of "water clothed by shadow and undressed by the sun," underlines the profound relationship which was to exist henceforth between the painter and his epoch. The visual problems that were to assail Monet in the last years of his life are perhaps the real reason for what came to be too simply called his tendency towards abstraction. Those strange canvases, conceived like *The House in the Roses* (ill. 112) in 1925 in semiblindness, were believed to be the result of a late adherence to a bent for nonfigurative painting. They really take one by surprise.

108 Claude Monet: *Hayricks near Chailly, Sunrise.* 1865. Oil on canvas, 30 x 60 cm. San Diego Museum of Art

The response of the Duc de Trévise is significant: "He shows me huge and disconcerting studies, made expressly on the spot, in the course of the last few summers, skeins of related colors like bizarre assortments of immaterial yarn." A cataract operation did not give complete satisfaction to Monet. Xanthopsy caused an exaggeration of yellows. The doctor's diagnosis, prudently optimistic, is most interesting for the information it indirectly gives on the master's method of painting. "M. Monet has more need of vision than of ordinary eyesight. His vision, such as it is, is fine for close viewing—it is adequate for seeing his palette at the customary distance, adequate also (we personally know) for making brushstrokes at his usual distance. But Monet, when he adds something to the canvas, steps back four or five meters; it is there (his vision of objects at a distance) that I fear I cannot now, and will never be able to, give him any help." It is odd that these artists "so obsessed with light," so thirsty for color, should be betrayed at the end of their lives by their eyes. Degas, who said: "A lamp is a problem, a sun is an insurmountable problem," went further and further into darkness. In his last years he could hardly devote himself to anything but sculpture. "The heavy lids," wrote Jacques-Emile Blanche, "droop over those eyes that were once so piercing, and which for quite a long time now have been able to distinguish objects only a little bit at a time."

"More light!" demanded the dying Goethe. The rise of Cézanne was also realized in full brilliance, that would haunt the generations to come. It would be, to quote that gentle poet, Rainer Maria Rilke, "reality raised to a level of indestructability, as a symbol of what continues beyond that which perishes." "Landscape cogitates in me, and I am its conscience." said Cézanne, and, "I am the aboriginal of the new art." Cézanne, also adopting the idea of the "Series," painted fifty St. Victors (ill. 111) in vain; the last one still did not satisfy him. "I'm getting old now, about sixty-six," he wrote to Emile Bernard. "The sensations of color which make up the light are the cause of abstractions that don't allow me to cover my canvas, or to follow the outlines of objects when the points of contact are tenuous and fragile; from which it happens therefore that my picture is unfinished."

Cézanne was never an Impressionist in the same way as Monet or Sisley. But the example of Pissarro, which brought a greater spontaneity of construction to Impressionism, transformed his palette (Pissarro was the only one of whom he acknowledged himself a pupil). "Until Pissarro I was dead," he exclaimed in 1872, with typical southern exaggeration. He tried at first to apply the precepts of the old master: "Never paint except with the three primary colors and their immediate derivatives." But it was hard for him to give up using black, and anyway he soon took it up again.

109 Claude Monet: *Hayricks, Effect of Snow, Sunset.* 1891. Oil on canvas, 75 x 94 cm. The Art Institute of Chicago (Potter Palmer Collection)

110 Claude Monet: *Hayrick in Winter.* 1891. Oil on canvas, 65.4 x 92.5 cm. Boston Museum of Fine Arts (Gift of the Misses Lamb)

The motive for the *Hayrick* series was not only the constantly changing weather on the face of eternal Nature, but also to focus on the hayrick in a series of "shots"—long-distance, middle and close-up, like a camera.

He did not have Monet's nervous brush or make use of Seurat's scientific partitioning; he proceeded by a building up of tiny strokes, a recurrence of touch and tone which gave solidity to the light and depicted the geological nature of the elements.

Cézanne's art, the fruit of frenzied labor, blossomed with the passing years. His diverse theories were harmoniously established in his painting. "Refashion Poussin after Nature," and "Interpret Nature by the cylinder, the sphere, the cone, all in perspective," so he recommended to Emile Bernard. More than ever Cézanne created a dialogue between light and shadow, form and color. He remade the world for himself and wanted it to stay that way forever. "Nature is always the same," he said, "but nothing that appears to us is lasting. Our art must give the thrill of the everlasting elements, of the constant variations. It must make us savor the eternal."

The sun illuminates, but it can also blind, and can kill in the long run. The sun in a Van Gogh picture has that formidable quality; it is disturbing. Contours bend in curves and scrolls that the experts know to be signs of madness. Van Gogh confided to his brother, "The figure of Christ has only been painted

111

112 Claude Monet: *The House in the Roses.* 1925. Oil on canvas, 89 x 100 cm. Private collection

The impressionist landscapes lead in many directions: to Cubism with Cézanne, to Abstraction with Monet, and to Expressionism with van Gogh.

113 Vincent van Gogh: *Starry Night.* 1889. Oil on canvas, 73.7 x 92.1 cm. New York, Museum of Modern Art (Lillie P. Bliss Bequest)

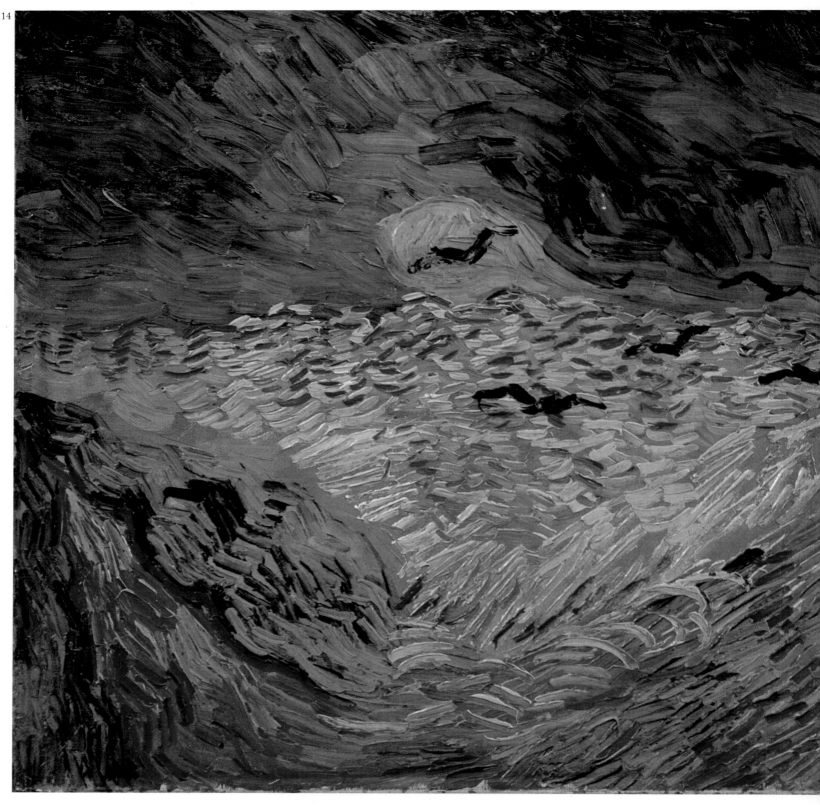

114 Vincent van Gogh: *Crows Over a Wheatfield.* 1890. Oil on canvas, 50.5 x 100.5 cm. Amsterdam, Rijksmuseum Vincent van Gogh

Van Gogh's landscapes are self-portraits. As in an apocalyptic vision the drama unfolds, imprinting its whirling rhythm on Nature. We can follow the evolution of the artist's soul in these flamboyant and sensational evocations

as I feel it by Delacroix and Rembrandt." But, "I have a painful need of (shall I say the word) religion. So I go out at night and paint the stars." But it was an apocalyptic vision that touched Vincent in *Starry Night* (ill. 113). The sky is animated with monstrous life, unrolling its gigantic tentacles, impressing its disturbing rhythms on the stars. In this hallucinatory work, the secret message of which neither Theo, nor Gauguin, nor Bernard, knew how to decipher, the artist is not less master of his vision, controlling the colors and balancing the composition.

"No, Van Gogh was not mad," wrote Antonin Artaud, his brother genius, "but his paintings were Greek fires, atomic bombs . . . after his passing nature itself, with its climates, its tides, and its equinoctial storms, could not keep its regular course."

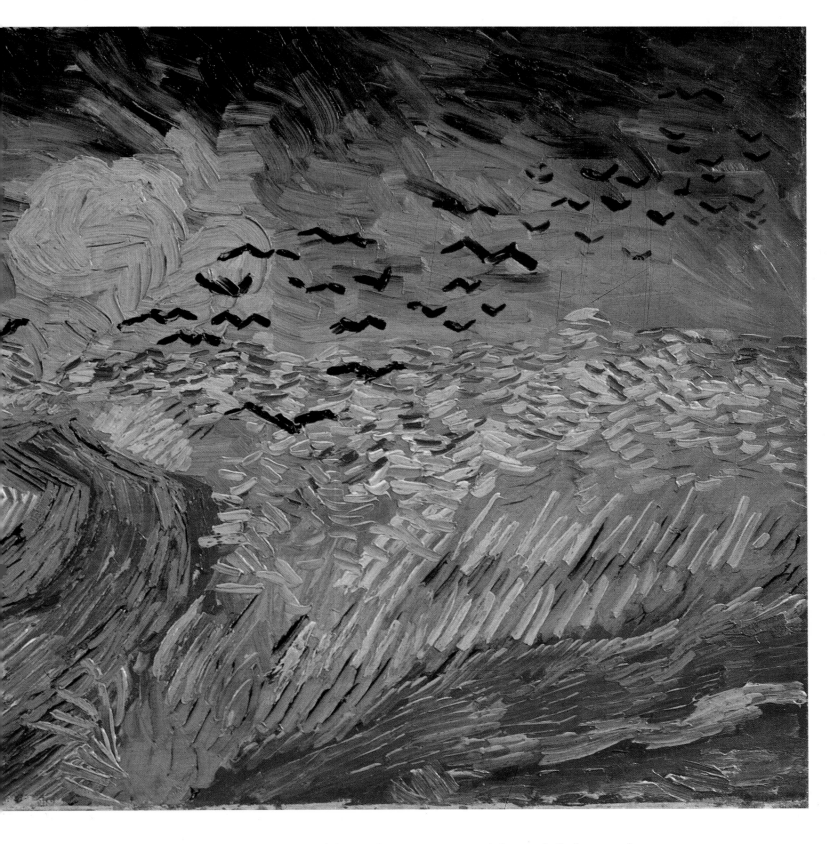

"As for my work, I have risked my life and my reason and have failed halfway," is written in a letter that Vincent was carrying on that fatal 29 July. "I cannot bring myself to believe that after *The Crows*, Van Gogh could have painted another picture." continued Artaud in his extraordinary essay, *Van Gogh, le Suicidé de la Société*. "Who has not already noticed how in this canvas the earth is the equivalent of the sea. Of all painters, Van Gogh is the one who strips us most completely, but as if we were rid of an obsession. That of making things be something other than what they are . . . And he has infused the color of wine lees into his canvas . . . I can hear the crows' wings beating like drums above an earth of which it seems that Van Gogh could not hold back the surge. Then death."

Nature would get the better of Van Gogh, the painter self-annihilated by his landscape.

from his inner self. He felt the fragility of mankind in the shattering immensity of the universe, something that was to cost him his life and his reason. He followed the black crows into his last picture, to die there, swallowed up by the monstrous landscape.

VIII   The portrait king

"Your wife, oh bourgeois, the loving and watchful guardian of your strong-box, will be the perfect embodiment of the kept woman," cried Baudelaire in his *Fusées*. "Your daughter, like a nubile child, will dream in her cradle of selling herself for a million."

Gauguin added: "Everything is rotten, both man and the arts."

The newly rich, the bourgeoisie, the sham nobility, and the captains of industry were looking for their cultural emblems under Louis XVIII. They sought a propriety which expressed continuity, stability, and eternity. The present had to be ennobled and the past made respectable. "All they had to do," said an ironic Baudelaire, "was to transpose ordinary, everyday life into a Greek framework." Such cardboard aristocracy was in the spirit of the times. Napoleon III confronts posterity in a photograph, astride a plush-covered stool (ill. 117). The beautiful Eugénie de Montijo de Guzman, the empress, with her maids of honor in their flounced crinolines and artificial flowers, seems to float like a ship at anchor before the easel of the German artist, Winterhalter (ill. 118).

The Russian czar, the Prussian king—with whom there would soon be war—and Queen Victoria, visited Paris, danced to the melodies of Offenbach, went riding, skated on the lake in the Bois de Boulogne, went to the Théâtre Français to see Sarah Bernhardt (ill. 120) in *La Dame aux camélias*, or admired Hortense Schneider in *La Belle Hélène*.

Ingres, president of the École des Beaux-Arts, senator, exerted an artistic dictatorship: Nature should be scrupulously copied in the way the old masters had done. His continual references to the past reassured the ruling classes.

If the Universal Exposition of 1867 had marked the high point of the Empire and confirmed Paris in her role as the capital of luxury and fashion, that of 1889, topped by the Eiffel Tower, celebrated in grandiose style the marriage of art and industry, while at the same time colonial conquests promised raw materials and new markets. It was the time, too, when elegant beauties (ill. 119) saw the first automobiles and railways, and the first photographs

> "A helmet is a hairstyle that suits them
> A fireman's helmet hardly makes a warrior."

The students of the *quat-zarts* celebrated ironically, chanting this ritual couplet, referring to the naked warriors wearing classical helmets that figured in the paintings of David and his academic followers. Even in a reappraisal of the conventional painters (nicknamed "firemen"), without prejudgment, it is difficult to contest the decision of history. One cannot deny the artistic superiority of Ingres or Delacroix over such painters as Bouguereau or Delaroche. Rodin's verdict is unimpeachable: "The ugly in art is the false, the artificial, that which seeks to be pretty or beautiful instead of being expressive, that which is affected and precious, that smiles without cause and feigns reluctance without reason, that struts and poses, everything that is without soul or truth, all that merely shows off, everything that lies." One rare perspicacious critic of the time passed sentence on Bouguereau: "I don't believe his palette was ever excited, or that his canvas ever caught fire when he put his overprudent brush to it." But the bourgeois always prefers the good student, and his taste for sweet things is revelatory of his own error of judgment. The newly rich, particularly the wealthy American industrialists, were already deeply immersed in art, and prices had risen accordingly. Luman Reed, an American grocer, spent a fortune on Bouguereau, Gérôme and Meissonier, carefully selecting those works offi-

115   **Pierre-August Renoir:** *Portrait of a Woman, Nini-gueule-de-raie.* **c. 1874. Oil on canvas, 32 x 24 cm. Private collection**

Renoir's first portraits were immediately successful. With *Nini-gueule-de-raie*, who had posed for *La Loge*, he resorted to a traditional enough craft, a smooth composition with the preparatory groundwork showing through the glaze. Here we see the milky flesh which was Renoir's alone. In the artificial light he found again the palette of his landscapes and their free brush strokes. Renoir was at his ease in anything to do with women and he used any means to portray their beauty. Fragonard and Manet had preceded him in that, and Picasso and Matisse would be similarly inspired in the future.

116 Paul Cézanne: *Woman with a Coffeepot.* 1890. Oil on canvas, 130.5 x 96.5 cm. Paris, The Louvre

Cézanne, said Valsecchi, was a new Giotto. His figures attain a rigorous geometry, a monumental majesty. His portraits seem hewn from stone or sculpted from wood. Cubism was on the way. The artist's ambition, avowed early in his life, was to make the ephemeral eternal, following the way of Poussin whom he admired almost as much as Delacroix. To create a synthesis between the perception of nature and the spirit of abstraction was not enough: He wanted to mix two worlds, that of Nature and that of the imagination.

cially recognized by the Salon or the Royal Academy. The czar of the American press, William Randolph Hearst, and the department store multimillionaire A. T. Stewart, devoted themselves to the fashion of the Salon. Stewart, like a good Yankee, bought a Meissonnier, the "prince of miniaturists," by telegram and paid $76,000 for it without having seen it. What a big thrill for the artists of the time whose prices were rising in the United States! The Americans bought so many Bouguereau canvases that when France wanted to organize a retrospective of his work in Paris in 1878, they could not assemble more than a dozen pictures. It was especially vexing for the museums that they had to go to the United States for this purpose.

In her work on decorative art, edited in 1897 in collaboration with the architect Ogden Codman, Edith Wharton stated that if the taste of the wealthy could be improved, the general level would automatically rise along with it. "That presupposes," commented James Harding, "that the taste of the rich is used as a reference, that people imitate it, and that the rich have bad taste. In order to take this into consideration it was necessary to retrace the great feats of the past and express their emotions." The hierarchical order of subjects was firmly established. Classical antiquity and mythology were at the top, followed in diminishing order by history—battles, naval combat—then affecting and moral scenes of contemporary life—medicine and scientific subjects being particularly esteemed. Then followed religious subjects and portraits—with the sitter's best features emphasized—and, at the very bottom, landscapes and still life, considered to be minor genres. In order to win the Prix de Rome, it was absolutely necessary to depict classical history, mythology, or the Bible. The commissions which came from the State were naturally for classical subjects of a high moral tone, glorious episodes from French history, etc. These glories had their museum, a veritable elephant cemetery, founded at Versailles by Louis-Philippe; however, occasionally in a corner of it a work by Gros, Delacroix, or David might be discovered.

Gleyre, an easygoing neoclassical painter, reminded his students: "When you draw a figure, young man, you must always think of the classical. Nature, my dear fellow, is all right as an element of study, but it offers nothing of interest. There is only style, you see."

"From that fabled coupling of the slug and the peacock, might have been born this thing known as M. Courbet." Thus Alexandre Dumas nicely expressed the disdain that intellectuals held him in. Courbet, however, who was to be publicly damned as "leader of the base and vulgar school," and who was to clear the ground for the Impressionists, began his career if not meekly, then in a very orthodox fashion. "I have at last been accepted for the exhibition," he wrote to his parents in March 1844, in connection with *Portrait of the Artist, Courbet, with a Black Dog.* "They have paid me the honor of giving me a very good place." To his grandfather he added that he would have got a medal if the picture had been larger. "It would have been a terrific début." Courbet, who came to Paris in 1840, was a frequent visitor to the Louvre. Except for Veronese, all Italian painting and its heirs "is shit," he said, with his Franche-Comté accent, which he liked to exaggerate. Modesty was not his forte, but the fact that in 1844 he could offer to the Salon three works as accomplished as the self-portrait, *Lovers in the Country,* and *The Hammock,* means that there was at least something to be said for him. He painted the portrait of Baudelaire, as a study for *The Studio*; he painted himself, pipe in mouth. He liked himself very much, and his contemporary, Théophile Silvestre, did not miss the occasion to remark, "In its last migration the soul of Narcissus came to rest in him. He paints himself in his pictures with much enjoyment and swoons with admiration for his own work." Others pointed out similarities with Caravaggio and Rembrandt. As for Courbet himself, he wrote to Bruyas, his friend and collector who had just bought a picture, that "he had just excaped from the barbarians. It's a miracle that in such difficult times I have had the courage to refuse two million francs from Napoleon." Actually, at the time of the Salon of 1851 Courbet haughtily refused Louis Napoleon's offer and asked double. He did not hang back from organizing a one-man show, and with this exploit he asserted himself as the third of the trio along with Delacroix and Ingres—the Realist opposing the Romanticist and the Classicist. There he showed his famous *Studio* (ill. 121). "I

117
looked at it for nearly an hour," wrote Delacroix, "and discovered a masterpiece." His only criticism was that the center of the painting is ambiguous; "It looks like a real sky." It was said of *The Studio* that it was *Las Meninas* without any king other than Courbet himself. He tried to explain what he had attempted to do in this huge "mishmash." "On the right are friends, workers, and connoisseurs of art. On the left is the other world of the people, of misery and poverty and wealth, of the exploiters and the exploited, those who live on death."

These *Studios*, whether by Courbet, Bazille (ill. 122) or Fantin-Latour (ill. 123), are declarations of intent and also an occasion for friends of the same group to be reunited elsewhere than at the café Guerbois. They make interest-

117   Napoleon III posing for a photograph for an equestrian picture. Paris, Bibliothèque nationale

During the Second Empire the fashion was for the antique. "We shall soon see antique children playing with antique balls and hoops and dolls and toys" said Baudelaire ironically. Monet's teacher, Gleyre, announced that "Praxiteles took the best parts of a hundred imperfect models in order to create a masterpiece. Whatever you do, think classically!" In this atmosphere Napoleon III posed for posterity through photography, that new painter of royalty. Probably, if he had dared, he would have posed naked, wearing a shining helmet and brandishing his scepter. The Empress Eugénie and her ladies-in-waiting gathered like galleons loaded with gold for the official portrait-painter of the Court, Winterhalter.

118

ing witnesses to an epoch. They are the hinge connecting the past and the new pictorial revolution. *A Studio in the Batignolles Quarter* by Fantin-Latour especially shows the influence of Manet on the young generation and emphasizes his role as guide. Both painters and critics are united by their taste for the naturalist vision, their desire to be of their own time, and by their contempt for academic claims. A fine gallery of portraits allows us to identify from left to right: Schölderer, Manet, Renoir, Astruc, Zola, Maître, Bazille, and Monet. Only the most bucolic painters are absent: Pissarro, Sisley, and Cézanne, always the less assiduous at Parisian reunions. In the following decade Manet would yield first place to Monet, who appears here in the background.

118 Léon Noël. *The Empress Eugénie and her Ladies-in-Waiting.* c. 1853. Lithograph after the picture by Franz Xavier Winterhalter. Paris, Bibliothèque nationale

119

Obviously, it is to Manet again that we owe this revolution. In response to the 120 painting which preceded him, burdened with literature, philosophy, or the socialism of Courbet, Manet offered painting brought back to itself, freed from all outside concerns. Its subject is of no consequence. For example, the arrival in Paris of a Spanish ballet troupe served as the excuse for *Lola de Valence* (ill. 127). With her magnificent costume sparkling with a thousand sequins, the picture is made. What is important is the happy coloration of multihued dots among which we see black, given its color value again by Manet. Baudelaire, scarcely a fan of Manet, recognized its importance and dedicated a famous quatrain to this masterpiece. There are two opposing styles in this portrait, the traditional style, smooth and finished, and the school of the dot or fleck. Obviously, the latter prevails and makes the painting cry out for attention. Manet, however, tried to follow the fashion. His Spanishness at the time when Napoleon III had married an Iberian beauty was sure to please. But he was not a courtier and his espousal of Spanishness was quite sincere. Since his journey to Vienna in 1856 he had been completely bowled over by Velasquez. Before the magnificent portraits sent by Philip IV to the Viennese court, Manet realized with what prodigious economy of means the painter of *Las Meninas*, by a judicious management of the brush, could obtain such an intensity of color with very few tones. Manet clearly retained this lesson from Velasquez; he understood that the greatest colorists are those who know how to control color. "How very Spanish!" Courbet was to exclaim some years later before some Manet works of that period, rejected by the Salon and assembled in a shed.

It suffices to bring together two portraits like that of *M. & Mme. Auguste Manet* (ill. 124) of 1860 and *Young Girl Leaning on an Urn* (ill. 125) of 1880, to understand that the break had been made. The first is still from the Couture period, that of his teacher, while the other is a true Manet, and what a distance there is between the two. In the first, Manet still feels obliged to make a likeness, but with no allowances. The father has a peevish air (perhaps because his son had become an artist rather than an admiral of the fleet), the mother seems submissive. Jacques Emile-Blanche, who knew them, said that they did not deserve to be transformed into a pair of concierges, and Léon Lagrange, columnist for the *Gazette des Beaux-Arts*, said of Manet in regard to this picture—exhibited at the Salon of 1861, and winner of an honorable mention— that he was a "portrait painter without any pity." The second painting is rapidly sketched in, brushed into place with large sweeps of the brush, the paint very thin, mixed with a dilutant, to capture the instantaneous effect, the feeling of life. "Here is a character among this crowd of eunuchs," Zola would say.

Manet was defended by Zola in the *Revue du XIXe siècle*. The painter thanked him and painted his portrait. Like that of Duranty by Degas or of Gustave Geffroy by Cézanne, it is a portrait which owes nothing to order. The Utamaro print, the etching from Goya's *Los Borrachos* and the *Olympia* that decorate the back wall add up to a veritable manifesto. Manet explained: "My sources are from Japan and Spain, but my aim is modern painting." The composition is a little uncertain, the pose stiff, the jacket puffed up. The pitiless critics commented: "The accessories are not in the foreground, the trousers are not made of fabric." Olivier Merson, a conventional painter, wrote disdainfully in *L'Année illustrée*: "It's unfortunate that the artist has not yet learned how to draw or paint."

Théophile Gautier butchered *The Woman with a Parrot*: "The head which M. Manet shows us is certainly an ugly likeness. On the vulgar and poorly drawn features is spread an earthy color that does not represent the coloring of a blonde young woman." Nevertheless, this was the kind of painting that would make the work of Gauguin, Cézanne, and Matisse possible.

The *Portrait of Théodore Duret* is much less constrained, happier and more natural, a symphony of blacks that sets off the famous yellow, so beloved of Manet. Duret, a journalist who had supported him from the beginning, tells of the picture's origin: "Manet wasn't happy with it. He put a stool near me and began to paint its garnet colored top. Then he had the idea of taking a paperbound book which he threw onto the stool and painted its bright green color. Then he put a lacquer tray on the stool, with a carafe, a glass, and a knife. All these objects added different tones in one corner of the picture. Then he

119 Emile-Auguste Carolus-Duran: *Lady with a Glove (The Artist's Wife)*. 1869. Oil on canvas, 228 x 164 cm. Paris, Musée d'Orsay

120 Georges-Jules-Victor Clairin: *Sarah Bernhardt*. 1879. Oil on canvas, 184.5 x 103.5 cm. Paris, Comédie-Française Collection

The academic painters, in spite of their fake Realism, their glossy Orientalism and trumpery Spanishness, sometimes produced virtuoso portraits. *The Lady with a Glove*, justly celebrated for its composition and coloring, brought its creator such success that he was over-whelmed with commissions and became the most sought-after portraitist—in spite of the fact that he would have preferred to depict the classical world. Clairin, a mediocre painter of historical subjects, immortalized Sarah Bernhardt in his portrait.

added something unexpected, a lemon on the glass on the little tray. Then I understood that I had seen enacted before me his instinctive way of seeing and feeling."

Manet is present again in *The Balcony* (ill. 128), but there is also something there of the naïveté of the Douanier Rousseau. In the foreground, and in the limelight, is Berthe Morisot, dear to the heart of Manet (ill. 129). He gave Berthe painting lessons and often used her as a model. It seems there was a mutual attraction between the two artists. With regard to The *Balcony* Berthe wrote to her sister: "I look strange rather than ugly. It seems that the epithet of 'femme fatale' has been circulating among the curious." The critics were spit-

121 Gustave Courbet: *The Painter's Studio.* 1855. Oil on canvas, 361 x 598 cm. Paris, The Louvre

Furious at his rejection by the Salon, Courbet organized what is today called a One-Man Show. Here is the Realist, opposite of the Romanticist and the Classicist, Delacroix and Ingres. "I stayed looking at it for almost an hour and discovered a masterpiece" said the former. Courbet wanted to make a modern allegory in this gallery of portraits. On the right are friends, workers, and connoisseurs of art, and we can recognize Baudelaire reading, Champfleury seated, Proudhon, Prossayet, Max Bouchon, Bruyas, On the left is the world of the people, of misery and poverty and wealth, of the exploiters and the exploited, those who live on death."

ting venom, as usual. *Le Nain jaune* wrote that Manet "has the habit of exasperating the bourgeoisie by his studied ugliness. But we look at it, we stop beneath his *Balcony* ornamented with two horrible bourgeoises in yellow gowns." Gautier, with his usual lack of perspicacity, said, "If he would take the trouble, he could become a good painter."

The reproach of ugliness had also been made to Degas. His dancers in their tutus are not altogether seductive. He never disdained to show grace in a form or a profile, but he always stayed faithful to the truth. The "little person," so graceful in movement, might appear awkward once the dance was over; he wanted to retain the expression of life, with its original flavor. "The women

122 Frédéric Bazille: *The Artist's Studio*. 1870. Oil on canvas, 98 x 128.5 cm. Paris, The Louvre

Mown down by Prussian bullets at the age of twenty-nine, Bazille has left us a moving testament with his *Studio*. On the walls are all his pictures. Over the sofa is *The Toilette*, while to the left is *Fisherman with a Net* (both now in the Musée de Montpellier). On the easel is *View of the Village*, which Manet is looking at, a hat on his head. The group of friends—we do not know if they are Renoir, Zola, Monet, Sisley—surround their leader, Manet.

here are almost all pretty," he wrote from New Orleans, "and many of them have that little dash of ugliness in their charm, without which there's no chance of real success." The posture of his laundresses and ironers, as they appeared in the small streets and shops of Montmartre, revealed the same sense of reality. We come upon them, glorious in their exertions, a heavy basket under their arm, or pressing on the iron with all their strength; or they yawn and stretch, a bottle of wine in their hand. There are no concessions to the conventional, either in the subject or in the composition.

While he was still a student, Manet had written in the margin of a notebook: "We must belong to our time and paint what we see." Degas had wanted to do "portraits of people in typical poses, and above all to give their faces the same choice of expression as their bodies." The one obtained his effects by color, the other by drawing. Degas puts his people among the furniture and other objects that make up their households, portraits become intimate scenes in which light plays its part in the glasses and mirrors—and on flesh: "I remember those feminine tints as ivory overlaid with pink, against dark dresses of green or black velvet." "To work on an impression of evening, of lamps and candles . . . the trick is not always to show the source of the light but its effect on things." Certain details, such as the embroidery of a fabric, or the carving on a little frame on the wall, are captured with the meticulous detail of a Dutch painting. But this same evocation of reality and life is also reminiscent of the Japanese. The Far East had been in vogue since the recent opening of Chinese and Japanese ports to western trade. The prints of Hokusai had been discovered around 1856 by Felix Bracquemond, an engraver friend of the Impressionists. If Eugénie de Montijo had made Spain fashionable—through Manet rather than through Degas—she had also contributed to the taste for chinoiserie by the success of a shop in the rue de Rivoli called "La Porte Chinoise," where one might meet artists and writers such as Zola, Baudelaire, and the Goncourts. Above all it was Degas who saw in Japanese prints the layouts that supported his own researches and confirmed certain discoveries he had made through his contacts with photography: he also found in them unusual gestures and movements. Gestures expressed personality and character, extending the individual and giving him spatial dimensions. His portraits show traces of this.

Manet never ceases to astonish us from portrait to portrait, nor to fertilize the seeds of all painting to come. *The Reading* is a portrait of his wife listening to Léon Leenhoff read, standing behind a sofa. "If his *Zola*," notes Germain Bazin, "is a farewell to the 'magnificent plum glaze' (Huysmans) of his youth, *The Reading* announces the arrival of his luminous period. Did he ever paint a more daring picture, with such lightness and spirit, white on white, like the famous *Duck* of Oudry?" It is already possible to conceive of the no less celebrated white square on a white ground of Malevitch. Above all, it is the intimacy of Bonnard, Vuillard, and the Nabis that this work anticipates. But what an immense amount of work it took to achieve it! Time after time he erased this or that portion of the painting until the result approached the visual perfection which he sought.

As with Ingres and the *Turkish Bath*, it was shortly before his death that Manet painted what is assuredly his masterpiece: *The Bar at the Folies Bergères*. These two works also have in common a boldness of distortion which was to influence modern painting. Behind the figure of the waitress—the most beautiful object among all those set before us (the lemon has yielded to oranges)—everything is unreal, reflected in the mirror. Perhaps this was meant to be a symbol of an ephemeral world; or expressive of Manet's philosophy on his deathbed, refusing to see a priest: "Everything is only an apparition,

123 Henri Fantin-Latour: *A Studio in the Batignolles Quarter.* 1870. Oil on canvas, 204 x 273.5 cm. Paris, The Louvre

Manet is also the star of this *Studio* picture, holding the palette. Behind him are Otto Scholderer, Renoir, Zola, Edmond Maître, Bazille and Monet, with Zacharie Astruc seated.

Fantin-Latour owes his reputation more to the floral bouquets he painted with such passion than to portraits. He painted roses "as if they were a woman's breasts," said J.E. Blanche.

123

124 Edouard Manet: *Portrait of M. and Mme. Auguste Manet.* 1860. Oil on canvas, 110 x 90 cm. Private collection

125 Edouard Manet: *Young Girl Leaning on an Urn.* 1880. Oil on canvas, 62 x 46 cm. Private collection

These two portraits are separated by twenty years—an eternity. In the first we see Couture's lessons still being observed in this picture of bourgeois comfort in which Manet grew up. The second is the true Manet, with its buoyant movement and expression. We pass on from the rather labored, posed picture to the swift brush catching instantaneous life.

a mirror reflection, the delight of an hour, the dream of one night. Only the painting of this illusion, reflection of a reflection, yet at the same time eternal, can retain some flecks of gold." (Germain Bazin).

There is a simple recipe for raising the circulation of an art review: it suffices to put a little girl painted by Renoir on the cover. Renoir's triumph was supreme with children. Up until then, he had been accused of "painting corpses and covering his figures with mold." Portraits as wonderful as *The Loge*, or of his model *Nini-gueule-de-raie* (ill. 115)—which gave him a chance to depict the beauty of a woman dressed to sparkle—charmed his admirers and crushed his rivals, but did not please "a public flocking in crowds but with evident prejudice," wrote Paul Durand-Ruel in his *Memoirs*. It should be said that *The Loge* represented Renoir at the first showing of the Impressionists at Nadar's. People "only saw in these great artists presumptuous illiterates seeking to make themselves noticed by their eccentricities."

His portraits in natural surroundings, like *Summer* (ill. 17) are no longer pleasing, though they are concerned with "flowers amid flowers." It is the Impressionist touch that makes the contours dissolve and the woman blend into the composition. In addition, the flowers are blurred.

Mlle. Georgette Charpentier, Seated (ill. 131), who appears in the celebrated *Portrait of Mme. Charpentier with her Children*, marks a turning point in Renoir's life; his material situation improved. Thanks to this bourgeois family, all of whose members he painted, his work began to be admired. In his report of

the Salon, published in *Le Siècle*, Castagnary characterizes the elements which constitute "the vivacious art" of the painter: "a lively and intelligent brush . . . his rapid strokes . . . that animated and smiling grace which makes an enchantment of color." In view of this unexpected success, Pissarro wrote on 27 May 1879 to his friend the pastry cook, Eugène Murer, "I think Renoir is now launched. So much the better! Poverty is very hard."

That masterpiece, *Luncheon of the Boating Party,* is the Impressionist testament of Renoir that "has gone as far as it can." After that he studied Ingres again and the decorative artists of the French eighteenth century. Such study gave a more exact form to his drawing, a more severe modeling. Jealous of Degas's pencil, Renoir disciplined himself, worked at his drawing, and tried black lead. His outlines grew harder and the figure stood out from its background. "I have gone back," he said, "to the old kind of painting, gentle and light, and I shall stay with it . . . It isn't anything new, but it's a continuation of the eighteenth-century pictures." He would leave it, however, but with *The Young Woman with a Swan,* for example, we see exactly the type of woman in whom he delighted, with almond eyes under clearly marked eyebrows, a slightly retroussé nose, and a rosy, pouting mouth like Brigitte Bardot's. Renoir now

Manet painted for the sake of painting. The subject did not matter, only the painting. The Spanishness of Lola de Valence was an excuse for painting the sequins on the dancer's magnificent costume.

A sarcastic journalist named him Don Manet y Courbetos y Zurbaran de Los Batignolles. Manet answered that his sources were Japanism and Hispanicism, but that his purpose was modern painting. On *The Balcony* are represented Berthe Morisot (seated), the painter; Fanny Clauss, violinist; and Antoine Guillemet, landscape artist.

paused to consider: at first he had gone to the limits of Impressionism only to discover, according to himself, that he did not know how to paint or draw. His return to classicism left him unsatisfied. He made a great number of rough sketches which he either abandoned or destroyed. His picture *The Coiffure*, which he had a difficult time finishing, did not please him. One of his achievements, however, was lasting, that which would come to be known as the "pearly" look of his paintings.

For a while, in his portraits, Renoir managed to unite the Impressionism in his backgrounds with the pearly brushstrokes on flesh and clothing of his classic period. Then came the day when, as his son Jean has explained so well in his memoirs, he sent all his theories to the devil. "Much more important than any theory, in my opinion, was Renoir's transition from the single to the married state. This restless man, incapable of staying in any one place, who would jump onto a train in the vague hope of enjoying the soft light of Guernsey, or losing himself in the pink reflection of Blida, had forgotten the meaning of the word 'home' . . . The arrival of my brother Pierre was to revolutionize Renoir's life. The theories of a new Athens were made obsolete by a dimple in the thigh of a newborn baby." Henceforth Renoir would follow his

126   Caricature with an Epigraph of Baudelaire. Paris, Bibliothèque nationale.

"Amid so much beauty which we see all around, I can well understand, my friends, that desire swings hither and thither; but shining in Lola de Valence is the unexpected charm of a pink and black jewel."

127   Edouard Manet: *Lola de Valence*. 1862. Oil on canvas, 123 x 92 cm. Paris, Musée d'Orsay, Galerie du Jeu de Paume

128   Edouard Manet: *The Balcony*. 1868-1869. Oil on canvas, 170 x 124.5 cm. Paris, The Louvre

129   Edouard Manet: *Berthe Morisot*. 1872. Lithograph, 20.3 x 14.2 cm. France, Private collection

128

129

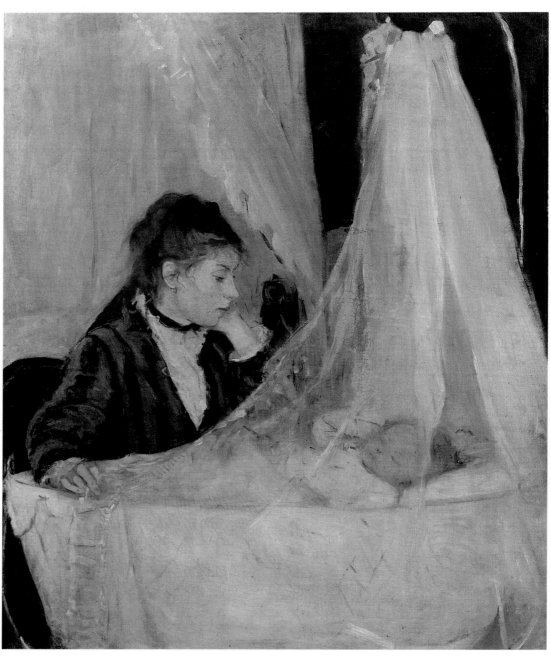

130 Berthe Morisot: *The Cradle.* 1872. Oil on canvas, 55 x 46 cm. Paris, Musée d'Orsay, Galerie du Jeu de Paume

131 Pierre-Auguste Renoir: *Mlle. Georgette Charpentier, Seated.* 1876. Oil on canvas, 98 x 73 cm. New York, Private collection

Who can resist Renoir's portraits of children? Even the critics give up and praise the painter's nimble brush . . . the lively and smiling grace which makes an enchantment of color. All the theories of a new Athens were negated by a dimple in the thigh of a newborn baby" said a well-informed witness, his son Jean, the film director.

As for Berthe Morisot, Manet's Egeria until his death, then a follower of Renoir, she dealt easily with intimate subjects; which assures her a place among the Impressionist group.

natural bent, to paint young women in their prime, come straight from Olympus with their bodies as supple and abundant as a Venus. "A breast" said Renoir, "is round and warm. If God had not created the feminine bosom, I don't know if I would have been a painter."

It was a similar instinct which guided Berthe Morisot, "star" of the fifth Impressionist exhibition, who would come under Renoir's influence after the death of Manet. The poetess of family life, she occupies a privileged place in the Impressionist galaxy. The singular thing about her, as Valéry has defined it, "was to live her painting and paint her life, as if it were a natural and necessary function." It is therefore not surprising, perhaps, that her masterpiece should be entitled *The Cradle* (ill. 130).

What a frightening mirror the self-portrait can be! An eye stares at an eye that stares at it. Rembrandt executed more than ninety of them in the course of his life. Some might call it narcissism, others see it as a message to future generations. It was neither of these for Rembrandt. He was rather ugly and knew it, and as a painter he rejoiced in the fact. The story of his life emanates from this series of self-portraits. It seems that each time he stood in front of the mirror, he wanted to make the point. His own experience was translated by the genius of his brush into profound and human truths. Therefore we can observe, as at a spectacle, the slow deterioration of his face, his attacks of melancholy, his sudden access of satisfaction or courage. We see him young, triumphant, famous at eighteen; we see him again with a double chin, the face creased with wrinkles that mark the ravages of the alcohol that kept him going and the ruin

132 Léon Bonnat: *Portrait of Léon Gambetta*, 1886-1888. Oil on canvas, 111.5 x 100 cm. Versailles, Musée national du chateau

133 Paul Cézanne: *Portrait of the Artist*. 1873-1876. Oil on canvas, 64 x 53 cm. Paris, The Louvre

133

132

Like all the academic painters, Bonnat had a brilliant career. He found inspiration in the Spanish school, studying in Madrid before working in the studio of Delacroix in Paris. And like all academic painters it is his portraits which have a certain majesty in their photographic likeness, in spite of too much bitumen and rather solemn poses. But we can see what a gulf there is between this sort of "good" painting and the arrangement of lines, masses and colors of Cézanne for whom the portrait was an excuse for the building of "a certain organic architecture where the living is temporarily rendered immobile and petrified." (Marcel Brion).

that lay in wait for him. A self-portrait shows how vulnerable its artist is, but it also shows man's capacity to survive and continue the struggle.

As with Rembrandt, each self-portrait of Van Gogh is also an accounting (ill. 134-136). That of 1888 which shows him with his easel—a setting which he borrowed from the *Self-portrait with Palette* of Cézanne—displays great authority and power, sureness in the use of color and the luminous accents. Paris had nothing more to teach Van Gogh, and from then on he was clearly master of his art.

During his time in Paris, Van Gogh was animated by a voracity for knowledge. Holland and social realism had not allowed him to resolve his problems as man and artist. In Paris, the place of his metamorphosis, he was faced with a lot of possibilities and he did not neglect any of them: Impressionism, Divisionism, Japanism, he explored all the avenues of contemporary painting, submitting himself earnestly to all their different disciplines. But being a rebel by nature, he only displayed his originality the more. Paris revealed to him the power of pure color, and he used it violently in the portrait of *The Italian Girl*. Just as Renoir had transformed his servant girl Gabrielle into a goddess from Olympus, so Van Gogh clothed *Père Tanguy*, a simple merchant, with the remote majesty of an oriental emperor. He succeeded in reconciling the veneration which he felt for this Socratic old gentleman with the decorative concepts

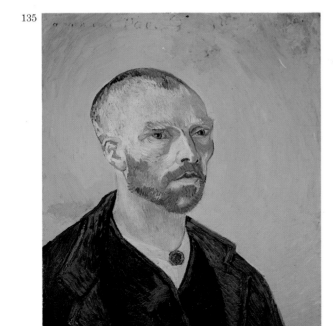

134   Vincent van Gogh: *Portrait of the Artist.* Saint-Rémy, 1889-1890. Oil on canvas, 65 x 54 cm. Paris, Musée d'Orsay, Galerie du Jeu de Paume

135   Vincent van Gogh: *Self-portrait.* 1888. Oil on canvas, 62 x 52 cm. Cambridge (Mass.), Fogg Art Museum

136   Vincent van Gogh: *Self-portrait with a Severed Ear.* 1889. Oil on canvas, 60 x 49 cm. London, Courtauld Institute

Van Gogh's inner life was so tormented and so intense that he was satisfied with only the architectural aspect of a portrait. His self-portraits pulsate with life, twisted like cypresses, flaming like sunflowers in terrible affirmation. Might he be called the brother of Rembrandt? They shared the same country, the same unhappy life, the same way of embracing the world and distilling their lyricism for our exaltation. Such a proliferation of self-portraits by both of them might be considered narcissism, but what a pitiless picture of solitude we see in these mirror-replicas or counterparts, disintegrating little by little.

of oriental art that he admired. The background of the picture is virtually papered with Japanese prints, which were Tanguy's merchandise, and which Vincent himself had collected for a long while. "Japanese art," he said, "fallen into neglect in its own country, has taken root among the French Impressionists . . . I envy the Japanese for their sureness and clarity. . . . They sketch a figure in a few sure strokes as easily as buttoning a waistcoat."

Antonin Artaud wrote of the terrible *Self-portrait* of 1888, "From the depths of his eyes, like something skinned by a butcher, Van Gogh gives himself up to one of his dark alchemical experiments which took nature for their object and used the human body like a crucible . . . Van Gogh's eye is that of a great genius, but it seems to me, analyzing it as it looms from the canvas, that it is no longer a painter's genius that I sense in him, but that of a philosopher such as I have never met in my life." Vincent awaited Gauguin's coming to the southern studio where he had kept for him this *Self-portrait with a Shaven Head*, one of his most hallucinatory works. "I conceived this portrait as that of a bonze," he wrote to Theo, "a simple worshipper of the eternal Buddha." Were there already signs of madness?

"I have now done a portrait of Dr. Gachet, with the heartrending expression of our times," wrote Van Gogh to Gauguin. "Something, as it might be, like Christ on the Mount of Olives, not destined to be understood." And to his sister: "I have made P. Gachet's portrait, with a melancholy expression that some-

137

137 Paul Gauguin: *Portrait of the Artist.* 1893-1894. Oil on canvas, 46 x 38 cm. Paris, Musée d'Orsay, Galerie du Jeu de Paume

Each self-portrait of Gauguin is like a challenge. At the end of his life he had the same eagle's beak of a nose, the same unyielding gaze confronting and overcoming the vicissitudes of life. Even when wearing spectacles (in his last self-portrait of 1903) the look is the same. As Strindberg said: "He is Gauguin the savage, hating a bothersome civilization . . . a child who pulls his toys apart to make others, one who repudiates and defies, who would rather see a red sky than the blue one the crowd sees."

times looks like a grimace to those who see it. But that's how it must be painted because only then, in opposition to the old contemplative portraits, will it have the expression of our times, suffering, awaiting something, and like a cry." Later artists, Edvard Munch the first of them, would take up this theme of the "cry" or "scream" and pursue it in their own fashion.

In Cézanne's portraits there is no cry, no feeling of the presence of God. Marcel Brion wrote that "a portrait is for Cézanne only a certain arrangement of lines, volume, and color, an opportunity to build a particular organic architecture in which the living is progressively paralyzed and petrified." For Cézanne, a face is the same as a chair or a fruit dish. We are far from any psychological analysis. It's more a geometrical analysis that he offers, as Raynal has noted, "by his interplay of angles, triangles and squares, in which the face stands out without sharpness because the artist draws with the brush." Cézanne did not seek to portray people's secret feelings in his portraits. The sitter seems to live "with a kind of elementary vegetable life." (Raynal) From self-portrait to self-portrait (ill. 133) the artist makes the image revolve and detaches it more and more from its background. It was as if he wanted to catch each facet of the face (as Giacometti would do later). His self-analysis is objective, like a certified report. His self-observation is keen, but his desire to simplify and abstract is dominant. "For Cézanne, art is a jealous goddess to whom all must be sacrificed." (Brion) He held himself apart from the storms of passion, and no metaphysical worries seemed to bother him. He was a man with one vocation: painting reduced to itself. With his portraits of Madame Cézanne, the artist removes himself further and further from the individuality of human beings, seeking only the solidity of the indestructible. His portraits seem graven in stone and more akin to sculpture than to painting. Cézanne had a long-avowed ambition to perpetuate the perishable by a method comparable to Poussin's— whom he revered almost as much as he did Delacroix. It was already possible to speak of Cubism, and to reject traditional truths founded on conventions held to be immutable until then. From canvas to canvas, Cézanne was able to synthesize two apparently contradictory forces—the perception of nature and the spirit of abstraction.

Woman with a Coffeepot (ill. 116) is the serene and majestic image of the wife-mother, extremely antierotic, whom the artist painted as if she were a Catholic Virgin. The vertically draped cloth gives the sitter all her majesty to such a point that one might wonder whether she is sitting or standing. Cézanne's difficulties with women are well known: he had only one wife with whom he never lived, preferring his mother's house as his home. This Virgin holds sway over domestic objects around her, and her face, seemingly sculpted in wood, appears to connect with them.

Toulouse-Lautrec neither flatters nor disfigures. He expresses whatever he chooses and if the cap fits, wear it; his implacable drawings take aim at idiots. His greatest mark of friendship was to paint a portrait. But he never overlooked the smallest wart and could aver without malice, speaking of a known rake, "He looks like a sole, he has both eyes on the same side of his nose." Many people were angry with him, and yet, under his magnifying glass, insects became unforgettable beings. How many graceless puppets, full of showy vulgarity, with flabby flesh, with primitive eroticism, given to us on postcards, have taken on, thanks to Lautrec, a quite different attraction? He was able to endow them with his own nobility, intelligence, sensitivity, and irony. "There is a feminine type of Lautrec's," notes Jean-Gabriel Domergue, "which he found by looking at living, dancing women. Like the Greeks, Lautrec had his gods and heroes, his painted idols." Lautrec set free was Lautrec discovering the lithograph. When he paints he still draws, setting a shape, making an exact expression. Once he learned the technique of the poster he only picked out the essentials from then on. Color is not there because it is color, but in order to emphasize a feature, underline an effect. He is the equal of the greatest Japanese—they are his kindred. His *Bruant* (ill. 140) is a counterpart of the portrait of an actor by Kunichika (ill. 139). Yvette Guilbert was the Greta Garbo of the 1890s. He made innumerable studies of her, particularly of the black gloves she wore, which fascinated him. She saw a caricature; he saw only a bird.

138 Paul Gauguin: *Self-portrait.* 1903. Black-lead drawing, 24 x 15 cm. France, Collection of Mme. Joly-Segalen

139 Ichiosai Kunichika: *Portrait of an Actor.* 19th century. Colored print, 136 x 24 cm. Philadelphia Museum of Art (Gift of Mr. & Mrs. Herbert Schimmel)

140 Henri de Toulouse-Lautrec: *Bruant in his Cabaret.* 1893. Lithograph poster, 127 x 92 cm. Private collection

"The Japanese artists strengthen me in my visual purpose (Pissarro). At the time of the Impressionists, things Japanese were very much in vogue. They attracted by their rejection of the picturesque, their use of pure color which nevertheless did not exclude the multiple gradation of color values. In Hiroshige's prints, Monet saw landscapes as bird's-eye views, flat tints without shadow or modelling, the decentralization of the subject, gestures arrested midway. In Utamaro, Kunichika, etc. Lautrec found one of the secrets of modern publicity—make schematic arrangements that grab people's attention.

IX   Venus or Nini

Plato had previously explained in *The Banquet* that there were two kinds of  Venus, the celestial and the carnal. Renoir was to put it more frankly: "A naked woman is either emerging out of the sea or out of bed; she will be called either Venus or Nini, and there is no more to be said."

A really erotic nude, as long as it was titled *The Birth of Venus* or *Susanna at the Bath*, could be publicly displayed at the Salon. It is similar to the distinction made in England between "nude" and "naked." The former means artistically unclothed, while the latter may be translated as "without a stitch on." Courbet's nudes are most certainly not nymphs. They give the impression that they have just got undressed, that in a heap in the corner of the studio are some muddy boots, some none-too-clean petticoats, and a frayed shawl. The academic nude, on the other hand, may be exciting, erotically spiced, even lewd, provided that it be of cultural or historical interest. It can be a reconstruction of something from antiquity (Gérôme; ill. 144), or the Stone Age (Cormon), a biblical or mythological scene (Bouguereau; ill. 141, 142), or even something from a French farce (Gervex; ill. 149).

Medals and decorations rain down upon those who know just how to arrange the draperies and poses suitable for nymphs or vestal virgins; who display just enough flesh in their martyrdoms to titillate the appetite of the lions in the arena and of the customers in the Salon. As long as they are called Bacchantes or Verities, these creatures may flaunt the most insolent bosoms, the most enticing rumps. The system works, even though nobody is deceived.

It would have been astonishing if that well-meaning young man Manet had not come to disturb things once more with his "gorilla woman," his "gamy courtesan." *Olympia* (ill. 150) is actually the first really naked woman, as real as the model taking off her robe to pose. There had been nothing like it since the *Bathsheba* of Rembrandt. The ambiguous symbol of the cat, the contrast of the black servant, do nothing to make things all right. Oddly enough, the work had been accepted by the jury of the Salon, but two guards were necessary to protect the painting from blows from the canes of indignant visitors. Discouraged, Manet wrote to Baudelaire, "Insults rain down on me like hail." Degas congratulated him in his own way: "Now you are as well known as Garibaldi!" "Manet has put a crack in public opinion," rejoiced Champfleury, while Paul de Saint-Victor commented, "The mob crowds in as if at the morgue, before the *Olympia* of M. Manet." He was accused of being a "brute who paints shameless women with a scrub brush." Although the composition was based on Titian's *Venus of Urbino*, it most definitely was not all right to show a prostitute in her boudoir, accepting a bouquet from one of her lovers—who might just have been going to visit the exhibition—stretched out, ready to make love; no, that would not do at all. Jules Claretie waxed indignant in *L'Artiste*, "Who is this concubine with a yellow stomach, some low model picked up who knows where, who represents Olympia? Which Olympia? A courtesan, doubtless. It's not M. Manet who will be reproached for having idealized crazy virgins, he has only made dirty virgins." Even Courbet was shocked: "It's dull and flat. It looks like the Queen of Spades just out of her bath." To which Manet should have replied: "Courbet's idea of roundness is a billiard ball."

The war of words would continue to range between the conventional artists and the Impressionists. Degas invented the verb "to bouguereau," which in his language meant to paint with one's feet. What did Bouguereau think of the new

141   William Bouguereau: *Dryads.* 1902. Oil on canvas, 215 x 280 cm. New York, Private collection.

142   William Bouguereau: *Nymphs and Satyr.* 1873. Oil on canvas, 260 x 180 cm. Williamstown (Mass.), Sterling and Francine Clark Art Institute

We notice here that despite his reputation it is not the satyr who is carrying off the nymphs into the undergrowth, but rather the reverse . . .

143

143 François-Edouard Picot: *Cupid and Psyche*. 1817. Oil on canvas, 234 x 291 cm. Paris, Musée d'Orsay

Picot was a pupil of David when in 1813 he carried off the second prize of the Grand Prix de Rome. He specialized in pleasant mythological scenes such as *Cupid and Psyche*, or *Orestes Sleeping in the Arms of Electra*. Thus he was representative of the post-David generation which prepared the way for the Academic movement. They enjoyed royal favor under Charles X and Louis-Philippe, who liked the way they dealt with historical scenes.

144 Jean-Léon Gérôme: *Innocence* or *Daphnis and Chloe*. 1852. Oil on canvas, 212 x 156 cm. Brest, Musée Municipal

No Prix de Rome for Gérôme, the erudite preface-writer of the *Nu esthétique*, but he got a medal for *The Cock-Fight*, acclaimed as a masterpiece and much praised by Théophile Gautier, who was to say of *The Balcony* by Manet: "If he gave himself the trouble, he could be a good painter." Gautier was much taken with *Innocence* and christened the new style "neo-Greek" or "Pompeian," for it was inspired in part by motifs from Greek vases and Roman murals. Gérôme devoted most of his time to doing battle with the Impressionists. Americans love his work and he was honored again in New York in 1972 by a retrospective organized by the Dayton Art Institute.

painting and of the Impressionists? He was not impressed. "Those people have no talent," he sneered. "They want to pose their models in full sunlight. What does a person do in bright sunlight? He makes a face; I do." To a journalist he asked: "Have you ever seen blue shadows? Do you think it clever to make women sweat rainbows?"

In the middle of all this brouhaha stands a curious personage: M. Ingres. All his life he wished to be classical and, not unlike Manet, his temperament constantly betrayed him. Even Renoir honored him, and not only in his "Ingresque" period, but before, at the time of the meetings at the Café Guerbois: "Corot was reproached for reworking his pictures in the studio. They railed against Ingres. I let them speak. I found that Corot was right, and I can delight secretly in the pretty belly of the Fountain, or the neck and arms of Mme. Rivière." Ingres, an orderly man, respectful of propriety and the established order, would have been much vexed if anyone had remarked to him that the sensitive and the sensual prevailed over the ideal and the rational in his work. "Here we find a navel that wanders off to the side, there a breast that points too much towards the armpit," Baudelaire criticized. His contemporaries did not hesitate to count the vertebrae in *Great Odalisque* (ill. 145), and it appears she had too many of them. "A woman's neck is never too long," said Ingres, who extolled the exaggeration of line, which he called correcting nature. "His nudes come from the light of desire," said Gaétan Picon very neatly. His wonderful bodies are unaware of the desire which they arouse. If their glances, their flesh, their clinging gowns are inviting, they do not know it. What could be more deliciously depraved! Degas, who in his youth had copied the *Saint Symphorien* of Ingres, particularly admired that painter's abandonment of the ceremonial in his big pictures in favor of the intimate pose, of nudity taken unawares, and himself pursued the path which led to his own *Women at their Toilette*. Matisse, who his master Bouguereau had once said would never be able to draw, admitted that he felt closer to *The Odalisque* than to *Olympia* of Manet. No doubt Ingres would at least have been surprised to see how far into distortion Matisse and Picasso would go as a consequence of the extra vertebra of the *Odalisque* and the goiter of *Angélique*.

130

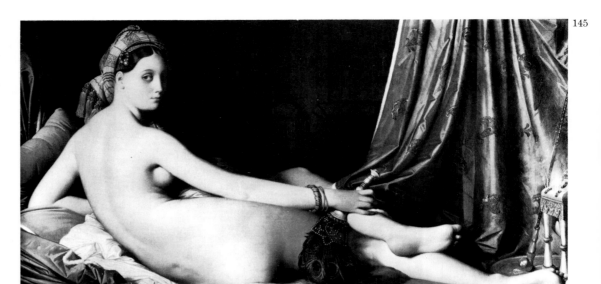

145 Jean-Auguste-Dominique Ingres: *Great Odalisque.* 1814. Oil on canvas, 91 x 162 cm. Paris, The Louvre

146 Alexandre Cabanel: *The Birth of Venus.* 1862. Oil on canvas, 130 x 225 cm. Paris, The Louvre

147 Léon-François Comerre: *Oriental Nude.* Undated. Oil on canvas, 98 x 143 cm. Paris, Private collection

Everything has been said about the three vertebrae too many in the *Great Odalisque,* which would give birth to the distortions of Cézanne, Matisse, and Picasso. Ingres differed from the Academies not only in his genius, but because he studied classical art in order to learn to see, not to imitate it. "Do you think I send you to the Louvre to find ideal beauty?" he said to his pupils. "That's the kind of thing that in bad times leads to artistic decadence. No, I send you so that you can learn to see Nature, because antique art is itself Nature." In turn, Renoir found the nudes of Ingres very pleasant, and delighted in his arms and necks and bellies. At the same time as he was castigating *The Bathers* of Cézanne, Napoleon III made Cabanel rich and famous by buying his exciting *Venus* for his personal collection. At the time, Philippe Hamerton produced this encomium: "She rests, bathed in light, on her bed of clear water. Beneath her tremble delicate rays of blue and emerald, and her long hair, like golden waves, is lost in the blue depths. Her voluptuous body quivers to the soft music of her exquisite form, her sleepy eyes are tinged with passion and her white arm begins to stir."

The eroticism of this canvas was recognized and accepted, also desired, as were those pictures having the pretext of Orientalism, since they provided an excuse for giving the public its ration of quivering flesh, as Comerre, represented here by an undated canvas, did regularly.

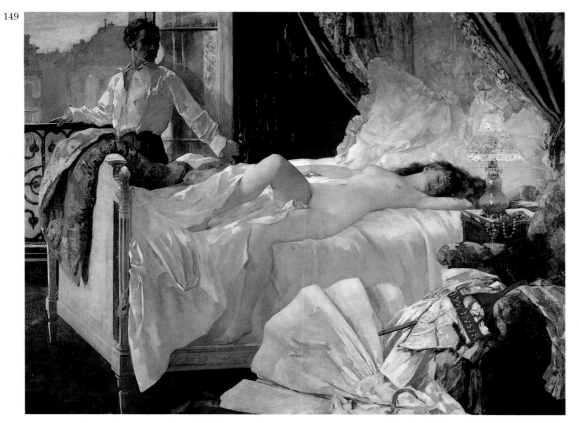

148 Gustave Courbet: *Idleness and Luxury* or *Slumber*. **1866. Oil on canvas, 135 x 200 cm. Paris, The Louvre, on deposit at the Musée du Petit Palais**

Courbet's eroticism was more subtle. The picture was commissioned by a rich Turk for his bedroom, but the Sapphic subject comes from Baudelaire, and Courbet has made "a poem about flesh, worthy of Correggio."

149 Henri Gervex: *Rolla.* **1878. Oil on canvas, 175 x 220 cm. Bordeaux, Musée des Beaux-Arts**

"Olympia's right place is in the Louvre" said Paul Valéry, "but I would put Rolla in my bathroom." Certainly with Gervex Academicism has united with Impressionism by way of Courbet's Realism and the supple effects of Manet's whites. On the advice of Degas, Gervex had wished to emphasize the realism of the scene by adding a pile of discarded clothing in the lower right corner. This one detail was enough for the picture to be condemned and removed from the Salon for immorality. As a portraitist Gervex was much esteemed by the smart Parisian public, particularly the feminine side of it.

Disappointed that Courbet had abandoned the painting of sociological themes, Zola scarcely recognized a single merit in him, save that of being a "flesh peddler." In reference to *The Studio*, the academician Henner was forced to admit that "a nude woman had never been better painted." However, André

The jury of the Salon had accepted
Manet's work without too much
thought. What a mistake! It took two
full-time guards to protect the picture
from the indignant assaults of the
aroused visitors. Critics and public alike

Fermigier noted that "*The Source* with her black hair, heavy thighs, and thick
ankles, is very much a woman of the Empire period, much more to the popular
taste than *Olympia*, who is more a goddess of the Salon." The subject of
Idleness and Luxury or *Slumber* (ill. 148) which was painted for a libidinous
Parisian Turk, is the same as the *Femmes damnées* of Baudelaire. Is this poem
to the flesh, worthy of Correggio, just a simple hymn to triumphant sensuality,
or is it, as some believe, the revelation of one of the Empire's hypocritical
aspects which he detested? "So will *The Young Women on the Banks of the
Seine* end up, though they also appear anxious," thinks Fermigier. "But the

150

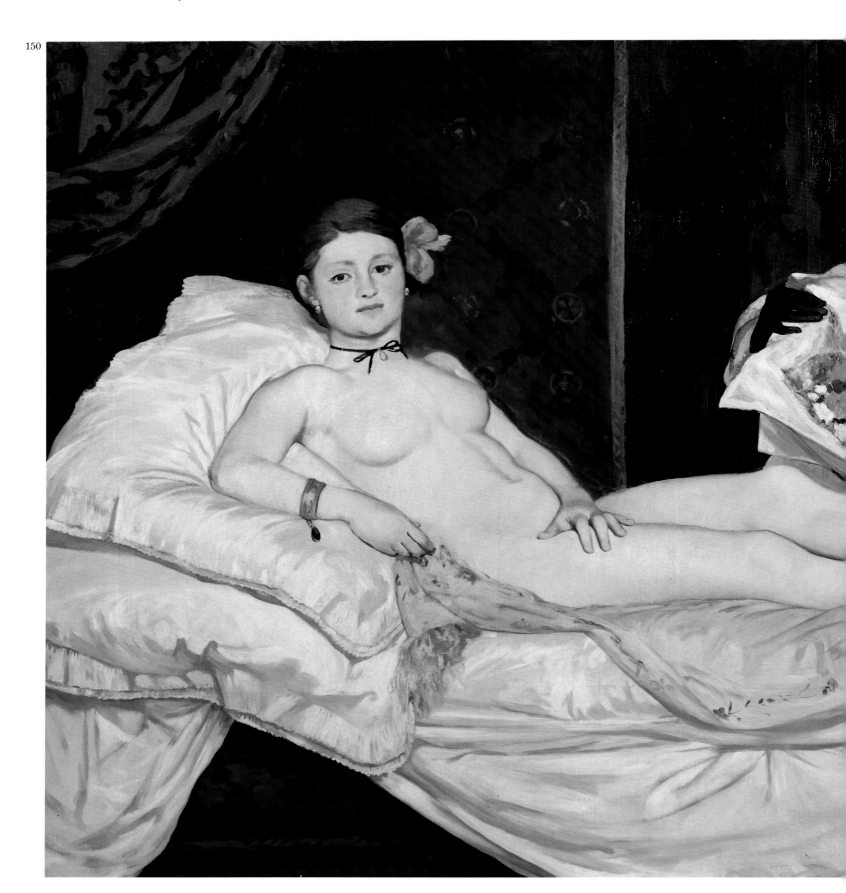

were infuriated by this curious creature, sometimes described as "a female gorilla." Up 'til now, all nudes, whether Classical or Romantic, had been more or less idealized. Now, with *Olympia*, here was a painter daring to present the first real female nude of modern art. There are limits which should not be overstepped.

151 Paul Cézanne: *A Modern Olympia* **1873-1874. Oil on canvas, 46 x 55 cm. Paris, The Louvre**

Shy, clumsy, awkward, taking inspiration from Manet, Cézanne mingled Impressionist technique with his recollections of Delacroix (his pyramidal composition). The man with the walking stick is himself, never at ease with women and dreaming of a distant idol.

152

MANET.
La Naissance du petit ébéniste.

152 Cham: *Manet, or the Birth of the Little Cabinet-maker.* **Humorous drawing which appeared in** *Le Charivari: Le Petit Impressionniste,* **1877**

153

LE PEINTRE IMPRESSIONNISTE.

153 "But these are corpse tones!"— "Yes; unfortunately, I wasn't able to get the smell!"

Reuse of a drawing of Cham done in 1846 in *Le Charivari: Le Petit Impressionniste,* 1877

Young Women were as stupid as goose girls, while the two sleeping friends are the very image of 'fearless pleasure' and no stigma attaches to them." A wide gulf separates Manet's *Lola de Valence* (ill. 127) and Gauguin's *And the Gold of their Bodies* (ill. 155). The second generation of Impressionists had succeeded the first, the generation of Gauguin, Van Gogh, Bernard. The first had favored the eye and nature over tradition; the second would claim "the right to dare anything." "I should like meadows dyed red and trees painted in blue," demanded Baudelaire. "Nature has no imagination." His wish was to be granted.

154   Paul Gauguin: *Exotic Eve*. 1890. Oil on canvas. 43 x 25 cm. Paris, Private collection.

When Gauguin the rebel returned to Paris, he did not fail to receive his admirers in exotic costume, flanked by a parrot, a monkey, and a mistress. "Those who reproach me don't know everything about the nature of an artist," he wrote in 1891. "Why do they want to impose their customs on us? We don't impose ours on them."

From *Exotic Eve* to *The Gold of Their Bodies*, his maturing freedom exploded. The artist wielded color without any attention to Realist custom. "What was important to him" notes Jean Clay, "was the psychological impact of a color, which added to his exotic nudes, evoked the feeling of Eden with unparalleled freshness."

154

Monet could say, "This hayrick is violet, so I will paint it as violet." The Neo-Impressionists went much further and demanded the right to paint it red if they felt like it. It opened the door to Fauvism and Expressionism. Van Gogh wrote in 1888, "Instead of trying to paint what is before my eyes, I use color quite arbitrarily in order to express myself strongly." This psychological conception of color would be used by Van Gogh to depict "horrifying human passions." In Tahiti, more easily than in Brittany, Gauguin could make a synthesis of form and color in opposition to the Impressionist analysis. "He is

anxious to know what you think about his evolution towards the simplification of form and the complication of the concept," wrote Mirbeau to Monet. He wanted to paint the Tahitian soul through the Tahitian body. He fixed forever the Tahitian type of beauty—a tranquil yet powerful nudity. Seeing a beautiful Tahitian girl one automatically thinks, "What a splendid Gauguin." It is this that makes us realize how the Impressionists changed the way we look at the world.

155 Paul Gauguin: *And the Gold of Their Bodies.* 1901. Oil on canvas, 67 x 76 cm. Paris, Musée d'Orsay, Galerie du Jeu de Paume

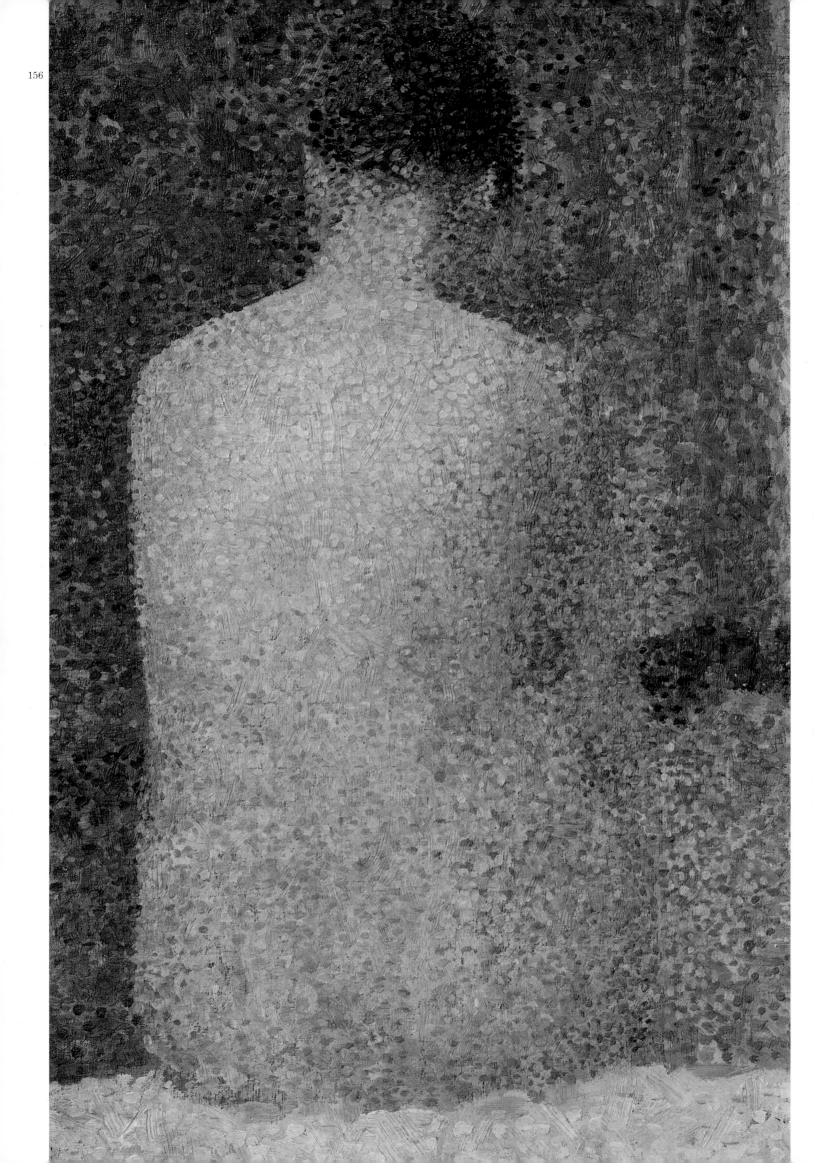

X Shrines of femininity

The sensuality and eroticism with which Ingres involuntarily studded all the works that we so admire today culminated in an unprecedented masterpiece which he signed proudly at the age of eighty-two: *The Turkish Bath* (ill. 157). This circular assemblage of nude bodies, all feminine, underwent a geometrization that the Cubists—via Cézanne—were to pursue, and later would influence "Pop" art. What a firework it is! Such incomparable inventive flexibility, a feast of audacity rarely equalled, a treasury: women offer themselves, perfume themselves, display their breasts, caress themselves or squander their caresses, intertwined. They are anticipating pleasure or revelling in it, their eyes closed, savoring the memory of it. At the end of his life Ingres reached the point toward which he had been tending for so long, bringing with him the sphere, cylinder, and cone so dear to Cézanne.

Even if the critics had been willing to admit that Seurat's Pointillism had succeeded with his seascapes, they would claim that the nude, and above all the representation of the human figure, were stumbling blocks for Divisionism. In order to demonstrate the contrary, the artist took on squarely the subject so beloved of academicism (ill. 156). His nude, moreover, would be a classical one in the style of *The Bather of Valpinçon* or *The Source* of Ingres. He wanted to show that a love for the pure line of the master he cherished and the Pointillist separation of tone and stroke could be reconciled. In order to leave nothing to chance and so that no one could say his success was simply good luck, he included three different poses on the same canvas, which is to say he gave himself three different problems. It is a real tightrope act we witness, very skillfully executed. As was his habit, Seurat made some preliminary sketches in pencil, but considerably fewer than usual, as if he knew what he wanted to do. He used exactly the same oil technique as in the seascapes of Honfleur. The first figure is in profile, taking off a green stocking. She has the noble grace of a classical statue. The second woman, seen from the back, presents a different problem and increases the difficulty. The usual outlines are not there. It is the teeming brushstrokes that in their closeness determine the shadows and vibrations of the flesh. In the final version, joined with a third standing woman, the figures nevertheless seem isolated, absorbed in their own world, as is always the case with Seurat. The picture was from the first called *The Model*, because it is actually the same model in three different poses. We are struck by the modernity of her shape. Profoundly different from the fleshy models in vogue at that time, the figure is fragile, slender, childish, ambiguous, the type that the cinema and fashion magazines have made popular today. "Ah! my dear brother, if I could only do something like it!" wrote Van Gogh to his brother Théo. On the other hand, notes Signac, "Renoir hates that picture; he finds it silly, ridiculous, and sees nothing at all in it."

That was because when Renoir painted a woman, he wanted her to be plump, not slender. The years of Ingres's influence had passed and he came closer and closer to the mellow curves of Boucher whom he had always admired. He developed a veritable hatred of Impressionism, a label that he had always rejected, and wanted to be a traditionalist. In 1882 he took up the subject he was very attached to, that of bathers, and began to dream of painting a large composition that would sum up the stage at which he had arrived. Inspired by a bas-relief of Girardon, *The Bath of Diana,* that ornamented a pond at Versailles, Renoir made a vast number of rough drafts, drawings, and studies of various details, contradicting the false notion, too often propagated, that the Impres-

156 Georges Seurat: *Model from the Back.* 1887. Oil on canvas, 24.4 x 15.7 cm. Paris, Musée d'Orsay, Galerie du Jeu de Paume

157 Jean-Auguste-Dominique Ingres: *The Turkish Bath.* 1862. Oil on canvas, diam. 108 cm. Paris, The Louvre

158 Jean-Jacques Henner: *Susannah at the Bath.* 1865. Oil on canvas, 185 x 130 cm. Paris, The Louvre

The painter, who after all is a man, has always revelled in his fantasies when painting feminine nudes. At the age of 82, Ingres dared to show what had always been suspected since *The Odalisque,* and *The Bather* or *Angélique,* that he had a pronounced taste for feminine rotundities, which he even put into a circular shape the more to underline them. Henner is not to be despised either. Between a *Dead Christ* and a *Christ on the Cross,* he wanted to show us a feminine type dear to his heart—a russet-haired nymph of olive complexion—a picture which was a huge international success commercially.

sionists always improvised according to their mood of the moment. In *The Great Bathers* (ill. 159) Renoir united innocence and sensuality with consummate artistry. There is nothing psychological in those appetizing forms. Renoir had always admired in Ingres's *The Source*, "that head that isn't thinking about anything." To an American painter who had come to visit him, he declared, "I arrange my subject as I want it, then I start to paint as a child would do. I want a red to resound like a bell; if it doesn't, I add more red and other colors until I have it. I have no rules and no methods . . . I must find what makes the flesh vibrate on my canvas." He wanted the blood to flush the faces, the arms, the hands, all the skin; they had to give the impression that they had been washed too much. Bathers, laundresses, or goddesses on Olympus? For Renoir, the earth was surely the paradise of the gods.

The Provençal poet Joseph d'Arbaud has told how one day Cézanne, with some constraint, asked him to get some photographs of nude women for him. "It will be much easier for you, a young man, than for me," he added, blushing. Too shy to issue a call for models, he preferred to shuffle a pack of photographs.

Cézanne said that he wanted to penetrate to the foundations of the landscape "and match the flanks of the hills with the curves of a woman." We might take this affirmation literally and reverse it with the scene of bathers, male or female—sex mattered little to the old master who only wanted to celebrate the marriage of the nude with nature—one of the most natural subjects, but one from which the artist would draw abstract-related, if not actually abstract, structural variations. Reality, which had furnished a point of departure for vision and imagination, becomes dislocated, is undone and remade according to the will of the painter who forces it to undergo all the necessary deformations to achieve exactly what he is seeking in the composition, and in which both the natural and the imaginary universes are made one. In Cézanne also, as a natural evolution, little by little the brain overcomes the eye.

159 Pierre-Auguste Renoir: *Large Bathers.* **1918. Oil on canvas, 110 x 160 cm. Paris, Musée d'Orsay, Galerie du Jeu de Paume**

There are no doubts or ambiguities about Renoir. The female body is the justification for the artist's work and is there to be touched. There is nothing psychological in these mouth-watering forms. Renoir remembered and admired Ingres' *The Source*, with its "head without a single thought."

159

That pictorial rite of Spring, *The Three Bathers*, reverberates like a manifesto of the Cézannian universe, all the fallout of which we have not yet discovered—Picasso's *Demoiselles d'Avignon* being not one of the least effects. The artist constructs it like the arches of a temple to femininity and nature. It is said that Cézanne, paying little attention to the models (he wanted to go beyond the nude as a sensual representation), had made use of a soldiers' bathing place that he had come upon accidentally. The nudes and the landscape become one, an overlapping that he explains better than any other: "I inhale the innocence of the world. A sharp sense of differences works in me. I feel myself imbued with all the nuances of infinity. I am one with my picture. We are an iridescent chaos."

Matisse bought *The Three Bathers* (ill. 160) at the suggestion of Pissarro and later made a gift of it to the Musée du Petit Palais. He wrote to the curator: "In the thirty-seven years I have owned it, I have known this canvas well—not completely, I hope; it sustained me morally at the critical moments of my life as an artist; I have drawn faith and perseverance from it."

160 Paul Cézanne. *The Three Bathers.* **1879-1882. Oil on canvas, 58 x 54 cm. Paris, Musée du Petit Palais**

Cézanne preferred to go beyond the nude as sensual representation. There was no problem about that. His picture was constructed like the arches of a temple to femininity and to nature. Thus, removed from the importunate cares of sexuality, we can celebrate the marriage of the nude and Nature. Abstraction will take care of everything.

161

162

XI Through the wall of intimacy

Lautrec's disappearances were very carefully arranged. He packed his bags and announced that he was leaving on a trip. A taxi was hailed to take him the hundred or so meters that separated Montmartre from the rue des Moulins where the "salon" of the same name held court. The move was made as openly as if he were taking the cure at a spa or making a retreat in a monastery.

There he was visited by Paul Durand, to whom he had given the address as that of his studio. The famous dealer, a rather prudish bourgeois, never related how Lautrec welcomed him among all the canvases and the half-naked boarders in this "salon." These were the scenes he painted which would subsequently be so proudly displayed on the walls of the museum at Albi. It was in that house with closed shutters that he finally "found girls of my size," as he jokingly said; "Nowhere do I feel more at home." There he was able to paint his masterpieces. The boarders were called Mlle. Popo, Mlle. Green Pea, Elsa the Viennese, etc. They were his models and they looked after him. "On Sundays," he said, "they play dice with me." An aristocrat from one of France's oldest families, Lautrec had never drawn any distinction between prostitutes and the nouveau riche. For him, aristocracy was a gift, a talent, and he often discovered it among what the world called "lost" women. He also liked the ambiguity of living on the edge of two different worlds. When the singer Yvette Guilbert asked him for his address, he gave her the notoriously well-known number of a brothel in the rue d'Amboise and was enormously amused by her shocked expression.

Once he was publicly asked by a man who was dining with his mistress and whose wife did not lead an exactly exemplary life, "How can you live in such places as those?" "Oh, you would rather have the scandal in your own house," retorted Lautrec.

There was nothing vulgar or lewd or equivocal in the scenes he painted there. On the contrary, what could be more terrible, more pathetic, than the picture *Solitude* in which a redheaded woman sprawls on a bed, alone and abandoned, ignoring the fact that her black stockings need pulling up. If, sometimes, Lautrec's women are preoccupied with themselves, perhaps it is because of the continual misuse they undergo. In his paintings, drawings, and lithographs, Lautrec's girls wash and dress themselves, take their breakfast, look at themselves in the mirror. They are not all beautiful, but they are something better than that—pathetic, human, and captivating (Philippe Huisman and M. G. Dortu).

Degas was appreciative of the intimate canvases that originated from this place (ill. 161, 162). "I can see, Lautrec, that you are one of us!" These nude women drying themselves, combing their hair, "It's the human animal attending to itself, the cat licking its fur," added the painter of dancers. If, for Degas, "Painting was private life," it could also be said that for him, as with Lautrec, Manet, or Seurat—and later Bonnard and Vuillard—his private life was painting. These painters seem astonished by naturalness, by a simplicity that they had not previously known. "It is the extraordinary privilege of art that the terrible, skilfully expressed, and grief, rhymed and cadenced, fill the spirit with tranquil joy," Baudelaire has remarked. With Lautrec and Degas, the horrible remains beautiful, and there is no distinction between pleasure and suffering.

Writers who were contemporary with Lautrec followed the same path and frequented the same places, Zola, the Goncourt brothers, Maupassant, and also the painters Guys, Degas, and Forain. But only Lautrec went beyond the pictorial anecdote. They called him M. Henri, the painter. Nobody was ever

161 *Henri de Toulouse-Lautrec and One of his Models in his Studio.* Photograph, c. 1894. Paris, Bibliothèque Nationale

162 Henri de Toulouse-Lautrec: *Au Salon de la rue des Moulins.* 1894. Pastel on paper, 111 x 132 cm. Albi, Musée Toulouse-Lautrec

To treat prostitutes like duchesses and vice versa, was a usual thing. There is nothing vulgar, lewd, or equivocal in these intimate scenes, which Toulouse-Lautrec painted on the spot. He was a discreet and considerate friend.

The common ancestor of the erotic magazine was called *Le Nu esthétique* and was published monthly under the direction of Emile Bayard. Each part had a preface by Gérôme, dedicated "to my venerated master and friend, William Bouguereau" and sold for one franc. They were full of spicy photographs, which were supposed to serve as artists' models. The captions mentioned the lens opening and the ASA of the film. Under the protection of the two Academicians, the magazine announced that it would show in each issue the beauty of the human body in detail. Each plate would show studies from the back, in profile, from the front and in three-quarters view, of stout or slender models, pretty or beautiful, of different racial types. Each issue would have four plates accompanied by a brief text.

163 Edouard Manet: *Woman in a Tub.* 1879. Pastel, 55 x 45 cm. Paris, Louvre, Dept. of Drawings

164 Edgar Degas: *Woman Doing her Hair.* 1887-1890. Pastel, 82 x 57 cm. Paris, The Louvre

surprised to see him; he could sketch whatever he wanted. He showed a photograph of two women clasped together to his friend Charles Maurin, the engraver: "That's better than anything," he said, "nothing could compete with something so simple." *Elles* was the brief title of the collection which Pellet, the publisher, ordered from the painter of the Moulin Rouge. That is to say women, those who either through obligation or choice paid with their bodies, and whom

Lautrec admired. Doubtless he discovered in their primitive spontaneity the freedom and truth he sought, finding the most perfect disembodied beauty in the most contemptible spectacles.

After the ethereal, delicate gestures of the dancers, Degas became interested in the compact gestures of women at their toilette (ill. 164). His dancers have the slender bodies of adolescents, representing young energy and the aspiration towards the ideal. The women we come upon in their everyday occupations have stocky, solid forms. So many contrasting possibilities confronted him. He captured on his canvases a very modern vision of the body in movement. His nude women in the process of their ablutions are seen as if through a keyhole, without consciousness of their beauty or the desire to get in the way. The painter's only aim has been to depict a body completely absorbed in itself, seen from an odd angle and with unusual foreshortening. Where do these seeming deformations and distortions come from? They have been called cynicism, cruelty, or misogyny, because people were not used to looking at a body just as a body, divorced from the idea of pleasure. But these distortions, even to the point of ugliness, help to make some of these poses as beautiful as those of the dancers. Antoine Terrasse writes that "Degas transcends the idea of realism or naturalism, and tends towards a new conception of the picture, in which form, movement, and color, all foster a specific unity." That is a definition that can apply to all modern art.

The painters were not deceived. Renoir and Pissarro admired this stage of Degas's work. He was now called M. Degas, as Ingres was M. Ingres. If the subject itself had lost its importance, as it had with Manet, if he painted a woman scarcely noticing that she was one, that was because he preferred to show movement and lines of energy. "Drawing is not form, it's the way of seeing the form," and "You must compose, even in the face of nature," such were the formulas that came out of the Impressionism that was so true to nature. He was particularly admired by the younger painters, Toulouse-Lautrec, Bonnard, Vuillard, and Maurice Denis.

165 Georges Seurat: *Woman Powdering Herself.* 1889-1890. Oil on canvas, 94.2 x 79.5 cm. London, Courtauld Institute

Always in quest of the new, the persistent Impressionists broke through the wall of intimacy. Not with any idea of voyeurism and still less for pleasure. Simply to take up the female body, busy with itself, as one might paint a cat licking itself. Woman without her various artifices, but getting ready for battle.

Regarding *Woman Powdering Herself* Pissarro said: "This poor Seurat's mistress is not wicked, perhaps, but she is certainly brainless." Madeleine Knoblock, who at twenty years old posed for this portrait—the only actual portrait the artist ever did in Pointillist style—certainly did not have much to offer Seurat. Of mediocre intelligence, profoundly ignorant, heavy of body, with vulgar features, she has been dressed up by Seurat like the cashier at a showman's booth at a fair, with her heavy gold bracelet, her showy earrings and her generous décolletage. In contrast, the composition is extremely refined, with marvellous coloring and hierarchical drawing. Fry would call it "abstract coloring."

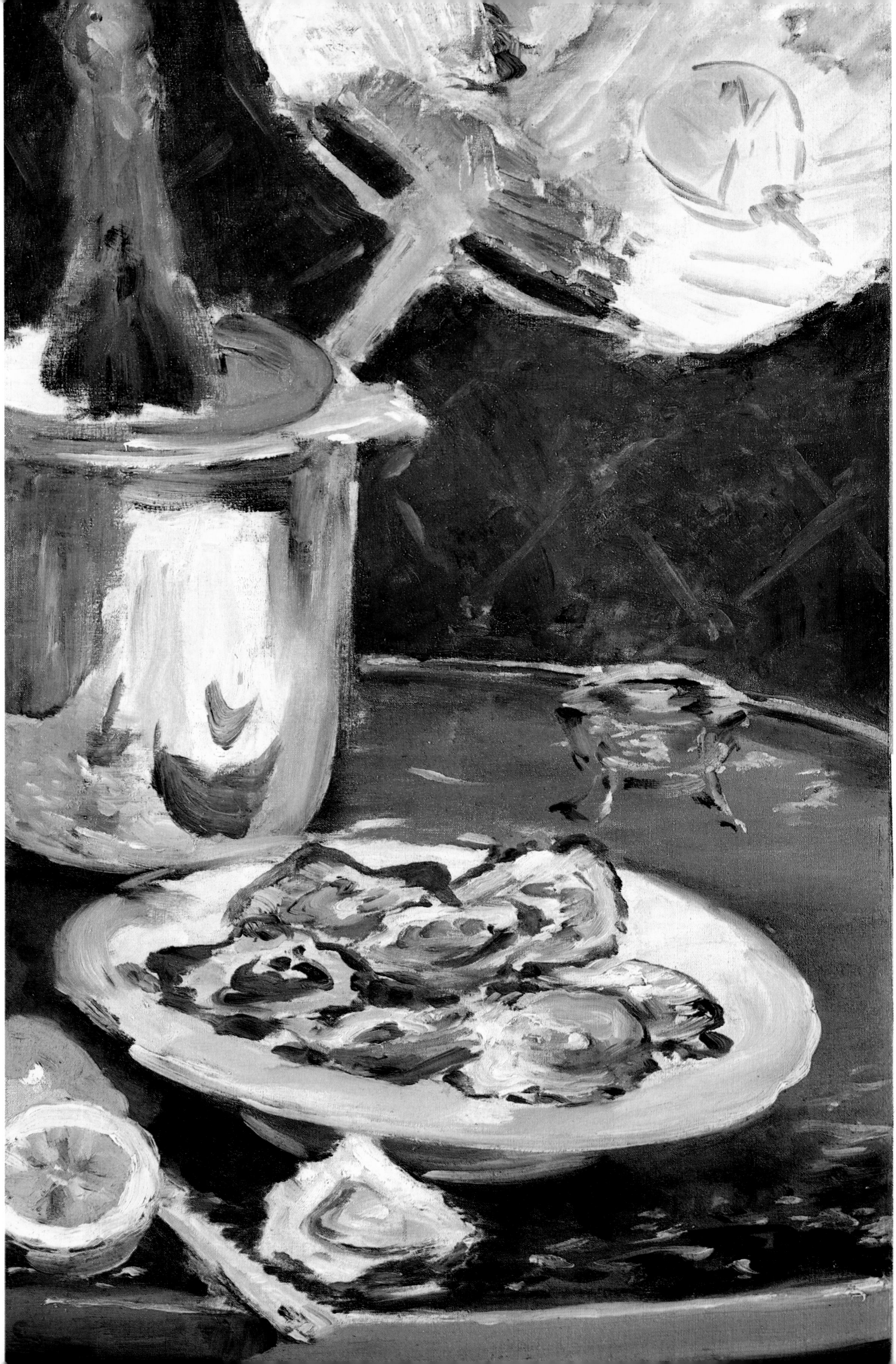

XII Still life

One might say of Cézanne that he was a "mediocre painter of apples," yet at the same time all Cubism and many other artistic trends were generated from his work. One might say of Manet—as of Giorgione and Caravaggio—that while he was not one of the giants of painting, he signified a decisive turning point in art, for one era ended with him and another opened. One of the most intelligent painters of his time, Degas, had a presentiment of it when, leaving the cemetery of Passy where Manet had been laid to rest, he said: "He was greater than we thought."

It is really with Manet that the great adventure of modern painting begins, freed from the necessity of telling a story and from false conventions. Matisse recognized him as the first to act by reflex, thus simplifying the job of the painter, to express only what immediately touched his senses. The moment he began to paint any excuse would do—"oysters and champagne" would suffice—and the result was a magnificent picture (ill. 166). A century later, Manet might have been an abstract painter. In contrast to Rembrandt or Delacroix, he rejected psychology and blocked off the secrets of the heart or the spirit. Hippolyte Babon said that he was accused of only seeing the exterior world as slabs or blobs, as if his eyes were dazzled by light.

The contrary position was held by Van Gogh who charged the least object with unbearable magic. His passion for *Sunflowers* (ill. 168) is partly explained by his discovery of "the eternal strong sun" of Provence, that mighty star whose symbol he would never cease painting. But, said Gaston Bachelard, "All flowers are flames that want to become light," and Van Gogh's sunflowers burn as brightly as the star they symbolize. They also open themselves like eyes in the intricate web of connections in which Vincent lived: they become the hallucinatory stare of the painter.

Drama is brewing between Van Gogh and Gauguin. On Christmas Eve, Vincent painted his homely wood chair (ill. 171) and at the same time Gauguin's most luxurious armchair. Vincent's pipe has gone out on his chair but there is a lighted candle on Gauguin's armchair. Much psychological analysis has tried to unravel the insuperable antagonism between the two men and two artists through this poignant diptych. The empty chair and extinguished pipe, as if left behind by a missing person, echo the lighted candle that seems to await someone's arrival. "Who is going to come in?" asks Antonin Artaud. "Will it be Gauguin or a ghost?" There are few works more tragic, more suggestive of loneliness and deprivation, than *Vincent's Bedroom at Arles* (ill. 172), although it is painted in vivid colors. "This time here's my bedroom, done very simply; only the color here is everything and in its simplification ought to suggest rest or sleep generally. The slight of the picture should be restful to the mind, or even the imagination . . . you see how simple the idea is. Shadows and projected shadows have been omitted, it's all done in flat, bold colors." Poor Vincent, seeking only to express peace, who waited impatiently to attain "the still life" (what the French call "nature morte," dead life).

Still life is not innocent. While he was painting courtesans, Courbet also painted hinds and roe deer, two aspects of the pleasure of life and love. His last deer, hanging by its hindfoot while blood runs from its wound, might be an image of Courbet himself wounded to death at the end of his battle.

166 Edouard Manet: *Oysters and Champagne*. 1877. Oil on canvas, 55 x 35 cm. Private collection

Whatever its name—*nature morte, still-leven* (Dutch), *vie silencieuse*, still life, Nature at rest (18th century), flowers and kitchen corners (*floreros y bodegones* in Spain)—each artist reveals himself in this genre, much more than in a landscape, as much as in a portrait. "A slice of life" the Impressionists called it.

It was through still life that the simplifying art of Manet laid the foundations of modern art. A stick of asparagus or a peony are as great as a huge composition. The subject doesn't matter—here it is oysters and champagne—as long as it expresses clear tones and a free brush stroke. We know that for the Impressionists the essential problem is the study of light. The masterpiece is free, offered as a bonus.

167

168

169

Gentle Renoir painted roses (ill. 167) while tormented by rheumatism. Gauguin, who had nothing left to prove, reached perfection with his still lifes (ill. 170). With *Le Repas*—also known under the title of *Nature morte fei* (fei means banana in Tahitian)—the artist demonstrates how his art found its real dimension in the tropics. Just this one scrap of painting makes Gauguin the equal of Cézanne in defining space and mass by color.

A painter of apples they called him! Those who think that is witty have no idea of what it means to paint an apple. On the day of his mother's funeral, Cézanne went to work on this subject instead of attending the burial. It was not the ill-mannered act of an eccentric. To paint was the greatest homage he could render to life or death. He likened himself to "an almond tree that gives fruit each season." Each picture is a step forward. A step towards the apple. In order to become "the pure painter" (Serusier), the "most painterly of painters" (Mirbeau), he went through diverse periods, Romantic-Expressionist, Impressionist, Constructivist, to attain finally the threshold of success, his Synthesis period. These were his stations of the cross, along the course of which he had in succession to free himself from the attraction of Delacroix and Manet; make "Poussin again from nature"; tear himself away from Pissarro, who was like God to him; then, without rejecting the lessons of Impressionism, build his forms according to strict geometrical construction so that he could finally reach that synthesis of perception and abstraction culminating in the apotheosis of light irradiated. This was a slow and complex alchemical process that allowed

167   Pierre-Auguste Renoir: *A Vase of Flowers.* 1901. Oil on canvas, 41 x 33 cm. Private collection

168   Vincent van Gogh: *Sunflowers.* 1888. Oil on canvas, 93 x 73 cm. London, National Gallery

169   Edouard Manet: *A Basket of Flowers.* 1880. Oil on canvas, 65 x 82 cm. New York, Private collection

170   Paul Gauguin: *Asters.* 1886. Oil on canvas, 60 x 73 cm. New York, Private collection

While the nude is certainly revelatory of an artist's obsessions, a still life is very much so as well. Renoir's roses are studies of flesh. Van Gogh's sunflowers are the burning sun. For Manet or Gauguin a still life was sometimes a pastime between great works, sometimes an occasion for the display of the latest techniques. Decorative and plastic qualities could be let loose through it.

170

Cézanne to achieve that "naïveté of vision" (Venturi) that did not intend to paint in a primitive style, but to return to original simplicity.

Cézanne's story is the story of an apple. It is one of the marriage of color and volume (ill. 174-176). The Impressionists had discovered that shadows were not black but violet. They had established the difference between "cold" colors, less stimulating to the eye, such as violet, blue, and green, and the "warm" colors, yellow, orange and red, all of which they used to render atmospheric vibrations. Cézanne went further and used these principles in modeling, to give the illusion of mass. Fauvism is only one of the early teachings of Cézanne, who wished, like the Fauvists, to make forms stronger by reducing them to geometry. We

171 Vincent van Gogh: *Van Gogh's Chair and Pipe.* 1888. Oil on canvas, 93 x 73.5. London, National Gallery

172 Vincent van Gogh: *Vincent's Bedroom at Arles.* 1888. Oil on canvas, 72 x 90 cm. Amsterdam, Rijksmuseum Vincent van Gogh

172

know the phrase that has been repeated a thousand times: "In nature everything leads to the cylinder, the cone, and the sphere." In order not to distract the eye with superfluous detail, he would not hesitate to make a face into a ball. Perhaps from the same source comes his fascination with apples, potbellied vases, and bowler hats. And the *Card Players* appear to be robots made up of spheres and cylinders.

But the greatness of the painter of apples is not only limited to his origination of Cubism. It resides in that irrational contradiction in him, his simultaneous love for geometry and for the indistinct, his confusion of vegetable and mineral. "The true forerunner," said C. F. Ramuz, "must be humbler, more uneven, more awkward, and meet more opposition." People speak of the clumsiness, the unskillfulness, the "touching sincerity" of Cézanne. However, nothing

The feeling of emptiness, of the void, makes one want to scream, and Van Gogh, who wanted only peace and quiet, arouses anguish. Everyday objects, the simple cane-bottomed chair, the room bright with colors, are attempts at exorcism. "I work uninterrupted in my room, which does me good and drives away abnormal thoughts," he wrote to Théo in 1889. Alas, the quiet he so much wanted was not for him. Few works are more simple or more tragic, few are more suggestive of loneliness and deprivation.

Gauguin's still lifes at Tahiti have the fullness and abundance of large compositions, the shapes of fruit and other objects being treated as definitive things, like architectural monuments, on the same order as Cézanne's works.

is uncalculated or not thought out. Emile Bernard said "Cézanne is far from being spontaneous, he is reflective. His genius is a flash of lightning in the depths." It has been said of his *Still Life with a Yellow Cushion* that it collapses like a house of cards. That is because the painter is no longer concerned with conformity or natural laws; he invents his own reality, the basis, nevertheless, of all modern art. "I will finish the pictures of that gentleman," said the Douanier Rousseau who felt himself to be, not without good reason, in affinity with Cézanne. But though Cézanne left blank spaces in the canvas, it was not through ineptness or lack of imagination, it was in order to make the stroke of neighboring color vibrate. It was the better to render luminosity and transparency. It was in order to infuse a mysterious life into inert matter. It was to

173

suggest movement through immobile objects. It was to make the apple seem to jump out from the linen that is the background.

This language of total independence, a severe solidity, was to transform the painting of our century. The Fauvists, the Cubists, the Expressionists all owe their existence to him. Although he lived in the last century, Cézanne belongs to this one. It is not possible to visit an art gallery nowadays without finding a trace of him. A picture several centimeters thick is nothing astonishing: Cézanne had already done it in his *Portrait of Uncle Dominique* or his *Portrait of Chocquet*. Today's distorted and splintered figures are nothing surprising:

174 Paul Cézanne: *Apples and Biscuits* c. 1879. Oil on canvas, 33 x 46 cm. Paris, Private collection

The "painter of apples" confronted with this fruit is like a child learning to read. "One must convey the image of what one sees while forgetting all that has been before oneself," he wrote to Emile Bernard. In his first attempt, with *Apples and Biscuits*, Cézanne attacks the fruit like a mason with a trowel in his hand. The brush strokes are thick, with violent contrasts between shadow and light. The white cloth is in strong relief and seems to push the apples forward to the surface of the picture to meet one's gaze. It is an instance of what is called Cézanne's inverted perspective.

175 Paul Cézanne: *Onions and Bottle.* c. 1895. Oil on canvas, 66 x 82 cm. Paris, The Louvre

In this picture, did Cézanne paint what the 18th century called a "vanity"? At this same time he painted, in effect, a heap of skulls in his *Three Skulls*. Sabine Cotte remarked that an onion has a dry look in contrast to the shiny look of an orange or apple. Might he have seen the onion as a symbol of death? The green shoots—apart from breaking up the geometric lines of the vegetables—are perhaps also a reminder that life comes out of death. Nothing is ever as simple as it seems with Cézanne. The bottle and glass are there to make a dark contrast with the color of the onions. But it is not by chance that they are half empty, the sort of thing of which the "vanities" often made symbolic use.

they are descendants of the *Boy in a Red Waistcoat,* with the long, rubbery arm; or the *Bathers* with huge thighs, with throats like cones and tiny heads, have perhaps come straight from the extra vertebrae of Ingres's *Odalisque.* Picasso sums up the exceptional importance of Cézanne thus: "In 1906, the influence of Cézanne, that genial Harpignies, was everywhere. The art of composition, of the contrast of form and the harmony of color spread rapidly. Two problems confronted me. I knew that painting had an intrinsic value, independent of the true representation of objects. I asked myself if we should rather represent things as we "knew" them to be, instead of as we "saw" them. We all know what happened subsequently."

176 Paul Cézanne: *Apples and Oranges.* c. 1895-1900. Oil on canvas, 74 x 93 cm. Paris, The Louvre

Here still life has become monumental and takes over the whole canvas, as Renoir's last portraits of women did. At first glance, we are surprised by this chaotic accumulation of objects, in which nothing is logical. Once again, the perspective seems inverted. The folds of the drapes seem to defy the laws of gravity. We are before a theatrical scene on which the curtain has just risen and which will only respond to its own director. But what we see is Cézanne's own inner world.

Such is the painter's power that he can impose his own vision on the laws of nature. Cézanne spoke the last word: "For development to be realized, there is only Nature, and the eye is educated through contact with it. It becomes 'concentric' by virtue of looking and working."

List of illustrations

Bazille, Frédéric (1841–1870)
Artist's Studio, The: ill. 122

Bonnat, Léon (1833–1922)
Portrait of Léon Gambetta: ill. 132

Boudin, Eugène (1824–1898)
Lady in White on the Beach at Trouville: ill. 81

Bouguereau, William (1825–1905)
Dryads: ill. 141
Nymphs and Satyr: ill. 142

Breton, Jules (1827–1906)
Gleaner, The: ill. 62

Cabanel, Alexandre (1823–1889)
Birth of Venus, The: ill. 146

Caillebotte, Gustave (1848–1894)
Pont de l'Europe, Le: ill. 58

Carolus-Duran, Emile-Auguste (1837–1917)
Lady with a Glove (The Artist's Wife): ill. 119

Cézanne, Paul (1839–1906)
Apples and Biscuits: ill. 174
Apples and Oranges: ill. 176
Card Players, The: ill. 75
Hermitage at Pontoise, The: ill. 49
Lake at Annecy, The: ill. 93
Modern Olympia, A: ill. 151
Mount Ste.-Victoire: ill. 111
Onions and Bottle: ill. 175
Portrait of the Artist: ill. 133
Three Bathers, The: ill. 160
Woman with a Coffeepot: ill. 116

Cham (1819–1879)
Manet, or the Birth of the Little Cabinet-maker: ill. 152

Clarin, George-Jules-Victor (1843–1919)
Sarah Bernhardt: ill. 120

Comerre, Léon-Francois (1850–1916)
Oriental Nude: ill. 147

Corot, Camille (1796–1875)
Rome, the Forum, View from the Farnese Gardens: ill. 102

Courbet, Gustave (1819–1877)
Idleness and Luxury or Slumber: ill. 148
Marine Landscape: ill. 95
Painter's Studio, The: ill. 121
Stone Breaker, The: ill. 65
Waves, The: ill. 94
Young Women on the Banks of the Seine: ill. 2

Couture, Thomas (1815–1879)
Romans of the Decadence, The: ill. 40

Darjou, Alfred-Henri (1832–1874)
The Empress Eugénie in Egypt in 1869 for the Inauguration of the Suez Canal: ill. 31

Daumier, Honoré (1808–1879)
Chess Players, The: ill. 76

Degas, Edgar (1834–1917)
Absinthe Drinker, The: ill. 74
Café Concert at Les Ambassadeurs: ill. 72
Dancer with a Red Shawl: ill. 71
Dancers Backstage: ill. 69
Dancers in Pink: ill. 70
Dancers in the Rehearsal Hall: ill. 68
Woman Doing Her Hair: ill. 164

Delacroix, Eugène (1798–1863)
Death of Ophelia: ill. 3
Liberty Leading the People, 28 July 1830: ill. 25

Fantin-Latour, Henri (1836–1904)
Studio in the Batignolles Quarter, A: ill. 123

Follet, Edouard
Marriage of Napoleon III and the Empress Eugénie (January 8, 1853): ill. 32

Gauguin, Paul (1848–1903)
And the Gold of Their Bodies: ill. 155
Asters: ill. 170
Exotic Eve: ill. 154
Garden in Winter, rue Carcel, The: ill. 20
Joseph and Potiphar's Wife: ill. 39
Landscape in Brittany—Willows: ill. 21
Man with an Axe: ill. 66
Peasant Woman of Brittany: ill. 60
Portrait of the Artist: ill. 137
Rocks in the Sea: ill. 91
Self-portrait: ill. 138
Still Life at the Comtess de N[imal]'s: ill. 173
Ta Matete (The Market): ill. 41
Women of Tahiti **or** *On the Beach:* ill. 22

Gérôme, Jean-Léon (1824–1904)
Innocence or Daphnis and Chloe: ill. 144

Gervex, Henri (1852–1929)
Rolla: ill. 149

Glaize, August-Barthélemy (1807–1893)
Country Picnic, The: ill. 7

Harpignies, Henri-Joseph (1819–1916)
Wooded Landscape at Sunset: ill. 103

Hiroshige, Ando (1797–1858)
Moonlight at Ryogoku: ill. 57

Ingres, Jean-Auguste-Dominique (1780–1867)
Great Odalisque: ill. 145
Raphael's House in Rome: ill. 101
Turkish Bath, The: ill. 157

Jongkind, Johann-Barthold (1819–1891)
Lighthouse at Honfleur, The: ill. 86

Kunichika, Ichiosai
Portrait of an Actor: ill. 139

Manet, Edouard (1832–1885)
Balcony, The: ill. 128
Basket of Flowers, A: ill. 169
Berthe Morisot: ill. 129
Execution of the Emperor Maximilian, The: ill. 24
Lola de Valence: ill. 127
Luncheon on the Grass: ill. 4
Music in the Tuileries: ill. 37
Olympia: ill. 150
Oysters and Champagne: ill. 166
Portrait of M. and Mme. Auguste Manet: ill. 124
Springtime—Jeanne de Marsy: ill. 13
Trumpet, The: ill. 23
Waitress, The: ill. 73
Woman in a Tub: ill. 163
Young Girl Leaning on an Urn: ill. 124

Meissonnier, Ernest (1815–1891)
Banks of the Seine at Poissy, The: ill. 87
Campaign in France, 1814, The: ill. 27
Seige of Paris, The: ill. 26

Millet, Jean-François (1814–1875)
Gleaners, The: ill. 59
Man with a Hoe, The: ill. 67

Monet, Claude (1840–1926)
Camille Monet and Her Cousin on the Beach at Trouville: ill. 82
Evening on the Meadow: ill. 15
Gare St.-Lazare: ill. 55
Grenouillere, La: ill. 85
Hayrick, Effect of Snow, Sunset: ill. 109
Hayrick in Winter: ill. 110
Hayricks Near Chailly, Sunrise: ill. 108
Impression, Sunrise: ill. 89
Parliament, London: ill. 52
Poplars on the River Epte: ill. 107
Rouen Cathedral, Portal and Albane Tower: ill. 54
Rouen Cathedral, Portal in Dull Weather: ill. 53
Rue Montorgueil, Fête, 30 June 1878, The: ill. 45
Waterlilies, Study of Water at Sunset: ill. 97
Waterlilies, Two Willows, Morning: ill. 99
Waterlily Pond and Bridge: ill. 96
Woman in the Garden: ill. 9
Woman with a Sunshade Turned to the Right: ill. 10

Morisot, Berthe (1841–1895)
Butterfly Chase, The: ill. 12
Cradle, The: ill. 130

Noël, Léon (1807–1887)
Empress Eugénie and Her Ladies-in-Waiting: ill. 118

Picot, François-Edouard (1786–1868)
Cupid and Psyche: ill. 143

Pissarro, Camille (1830–1903)
Boulevard Montmartre, Night Effect: ill. 46
Hermitage at Pontoise: ill. 49
Kitchen Garden with Trees in Flower, Spring: ill. 106
Pavillion de Flore and the Pont Royal, Le: ill. 47
Woman Carrying Hay on a Hand-Barrow: ill. 63
Woman Emptying a Wheelbarrow: ill. 64
Young Girl with a Stick: ill. 14

Pollock, Jackson (1912–1956)
Painting: ill. 98

Raimondi, Marc-Antoine (c. 1480–1534)
Judgement of Paris, The: ill. 5

Renoir, Pierre-Auguste (1841–1919)
Champs-Elysées, During the Exposition Universelle of 1867: ill. 48
Dance in the City: ill. 78
Dance in the Country: ill. 77
Gabrielle with a Rose: ill. 19
Madame Choquet Reading: ill. 16
Mlle. Georgette Charpentier, Seated: ill. 131
Portrait of a Woman, Nini-queule-de-raie: ill. 115
Summer: ill. 17
The Swing: ill. 1
Vase of Flowers, A: ill. 167
Woman in a Straw Hat: ill. 18

Rousseau, Théodore (1812–1867)
Wooded Landscape: ill. 105

Seurat, George-Pierre (1859–1891)
Bec du Hoc, Le: ill. 92
Model from the Back: ill. 156
Sunday Afternoon on the Island of la Grande Jatte: ill. 38
Woman Powdering Herself: ill. 65

Sisley, Alfred (1839–1899)
Flood at Port Marly, The: ill. 88
Fog at Voisins: ill. 104
Snow at Louvenciennes: ill. 100

Titian (1488/1489–1576)
Rustic Concert, The: ill. 6

Toulouse-Lautrec, Henri de (1864–1901)
Bruant in His Cabaret: ill. 140
Loïe Fuller at the Folies Bergères: ill. 79
Moulin Rouge, At the: ill. 80
Salon de la rue des Moulins, Au: ill. 162

Turner, Joseph Mallord William (1775–1851)
The Burning of the House of Lords and Commons, 16th October, 1834: ill. 51
Keelmen Heaving in Coals by Night: ill. 90

Van Gogh, Vincent (1853–1890)
Crows over a Wheatfield: ill. 114
Noon or The Siesta: ill. 61
Portrait of the Artist: ill. 134
Restaurant of la Sirene at Asnières, The: ill. 50
Self-portrait: ill. 135
Self-portrait with a Severed Ear: ill. 136
Starry Night: ill. 113
Sunflowers: ill. 168
Van Gogh's Chair and Pipe: ill. 171
Vincent's Bedroom at Arles: ill. 172

Whistler, James McNeill (1834–1903)
Old Battersea Bridge: ill. 56

Yvon, Adolphe (1817–1893)
Annexation of the Suburbs, 16 June 1859, Napoleon III Delivers the Annexation Decree to Haussmann, The: ill. 28

Bibliography

General Works in chronological order

Leymarie, J., *Manet et les Impressionnistes au Musée du Louvre*, Librairie des Arts décoratifs, Paris, 1948.

Raynal, M., *Le dix-neuvième siècle, de Goya à Gauguin*, Skira, Geneva, 1951.

Venturi, L., *De Manet à Lautrec*, Albin Michel, Paris, 1953.

Rewald, J., *Post-Impressionism from Van Gogh to Gauguin*, The Museum of Modern Art, New York, 1956.

Leymarie, J., *La Peinture française, le dix-neuvième siècle*, Skira, Geneva, 1962.

Blunden, M. et G., *Journal de l'Impressionnisme*, Skira, Geneva, 1970.

Clay, J., *L'Impressionnisme*, Hachette-Réalités, 1970.

Sutter, J., *Les Néo-Impressionnistes*, Lausanne, Bibliothèque des Arts, 1970.

Harding, J., *Les peintres pompiers, la peinture académique en France de 1830 à 1880*, Flammarion, Paris, 1980.

Blunden, M. et G., *La peinture de l'Impressionnisme*, réimpression du *Journal de l'Impressionnisme*, Skira, Geneva, 1981.

Clay, J., *Comprendre l'Impressionnisme*, Chêne, Paris. 1984.

Monographs

Paul Cézanne

Venturi, L., *Cézanne, son art, son œuvre*, 2 vol., Paris. 1956.

Brion, M., *Paul Cézanne*, Diffusion Princesse, Paris, 1974.

Taillandier, Y., *Cézanne*, Flammarion, Paris, 1979.

Edgar Degas

Valéry, P., *Degas, danse, dessin*, Gallimard, Paris, 1956.

Terrasse, A., *Degas*, Diffusion Princesse, Paris, 1974.

Paul Gauguin

Wildenstein, G., *Gauguin*, Les Beaux-Arts, Paris. 1964.

Cogniat, R., *Gauguin*, Diffusion Princesse, Paris, 1974.

Edouard Manet

Schneider, P., *Manet et son temps*, Time-Life International, 1972.

Bazin, G., *Manet*, Diffusion Princesse, Paris, 1974.

Rouart, D. et Wildenstein, D., *Edouard Manet, catalogue raisonné*, v. 1, *Peintures*, v. 2, *Pastels, aquarelles, dessins*, Fondation Wildenstein – Bibliothèque des Arts, Paris – New York – Lausanne, 1975.

Claude Monet

Wildenstein, D., *Claude Monet, biographie et catalogue raisonné, Peintures*, v. 1 (1840–1881), Bibliothèque des Arts, Lausanne – Paris, 1974; v. 2 (1882–1886), *ibidem*, 1979; v. 3 (1887–1898), *ibidem*, 1979.

Camille Pissarro

Pissarro, L.-R. and Venturi, L., *Camille Pissarro, son art, son œuvre*, 2 vol., Paris, 1939.

Kunstler, C., *Pissarro*, Diffusion Princesse, Paris, 1974.

Pierre-Auguste Renoir

Renoir, J., *Renoir par Renoir*, Fayard-Hachette, Paris, 1962.

Daulte, F., *Auguste Renoir, catalogue raisonné de l'œuvre peint*, v. 1, *Figures* (1860–1890), Editions Durand-Ruel, Lausanne, 1971.

Georges-Pierre Seurat

Dorra, H. and Reward, J., *Seurat, l'œuvre peint, biographie et catalogue critique*, Les Beaux-Arts, Paris. 1959.

Hautecœur, L., *Seurat*, Diffusion Princesse, 1974.

Alfred Sisley

Daulte, F., *Alfred Sisley, catalogue raisonné de l'œuvre peint*, Lausanne, 1959.

Daulte, F., *Sisley*, Diffusion Princesse, 1974.

Henri de Toulouse-Lautrec

Huisman, Ph. and Dortu, M. G., *Lautrec par Lautrec*, Edita, Lausanne, 1964.

Vincent van Gogh

Correspondance complète enrichie de tous les dessins originaux, introduction and notes by Georges Charensol, 3 vol., Gallimard-Grasset, Paris, 1960.

Artaud, A., "Van Gogh le Suicidé de la Sociéte", Paris, 1947; *Œuvres complètes*, v. 13, XIII, Gallimard, Paris, 1974.

Faille, J.-B. de la, *The Works of Vincent van Gogh, His Paintings and Drawings*, Meulenhoff, Amsterdam; Reynal and William Morrow, New York, 1970.

Zurcher, B., *Van Gogh, Vie et œuvre*, Office du Livre, Fribourg, 1985.

Photographic Credits